ALL-AMERICAN TRIVIA

Where History Happened

From Sea to Shining Sea

Publications International, Ltd.

Compiled and written by **Douglas Tonks.**

Additional writing and research by **Jennifer Huston, Alyssa Amedei,** and **Sarah Gorr.**

Image credits: JupiterImages, Library of Congress, PIL Collection, Shutterstock, Thinkstock

Cover images: Thinkstock

Louis Weber, CEO
Publications International, Ltd.
7373 North Cicero Avenue
Lincolnwood, Illinois 60712

Permission is never granted for commercial purposes.

ISBN-13: 978-1-4508-5008-7
ISBN-10: 1-4508-5008-1

Manufactured in USA.

8 7 6 5 4 3 2 1

CONTENTS

★ ★ ★ ★ ★ ★ ★ ★ ★ ★ ★ ★ ★ ★ ★ ★ ★

EARLY EXPLORATION

★ ★ ★ ★ ★ ★ ★ ★ ★ ★ ★ ★ ★

European explorers sailing to North America in the late 15th, 16th, and 17th centuries truly were expanding the world that they knew. Where were some of the most significant discoveries made?

Q. Where in the modern-day United States did Christopher Columbus land?

A. Nowhere. It's a common myth that Columbus sailed to the United States when he "discovered" America, but at no time in his life did Christopher Columbus set foot on any of what are today's 50 United States. He did visit Puerto Rico, however, and he also named the Virgin Islands. His only visit to the American landmass was on his fourth voyage—when he cruised from modern Honduras to Panama.

Q. What is the oldest continuous European settlement in the United States?

A. St. Augustine, Florida. Because Florida was not one of the original 13 colonies and did not join the United States until the 19th century, St. Augustine is often left out of a discussion of America's first cities. First spotted in 1513 by Spanish explorer Juan Ponce de León, the site of the present-day city was important in the colonial battles between France, England, and Spain. France sent a convoy to settle the east coast of Florida, right in the path of Spain's treasure ships returning home with

> *"Groves of lofty and flourishing trees are abundant, as also large lakes, surrounded and overhung by the foliage, in a most enchanting manner. Everything looked as green as in April in Andalusia. The melody of the birds was so exquisite that one was never willing to part from the spot, and the flocks of parrots obscured the heavens."*
> —Christopher Columbus, during his first voyage to the New World

plunder from the New World. In August 1565 Pedro Menéndez de Avilés, a Spanish admiral, destroyed French forces stationed there and built the town of St. Augustine—some 40 years before the British settled Jamestown, Virginia.

Q. How did North and South America get their names?

A. The continents may have been named after Italian explorer Amerigo Vespucci, who made as many as four voyages to South America between 1497 and 1504. On a 1501 trek, he realized he wasn't visiting Asia, as Columbus had believed, but a brand-spankin' new continent. He wrote about his exploits (livening them up with salacious details of native behavior wherever he felt necessary) in a series of letters to his patrons. German cartographer Martin Waldseemüller, a fan, decided to label the new land *America* on a 1507 map. But the first line above, however, said the continents "may have been" named for him. Some historians contend that the term *America* was already in use at the time and that Waldseemüller was incorrect in assuming it referred to Vespucci. No matter where the name originated, however, Waldseemüller's intention was to honor Vespucci. This map proved highly influential, as other cartographers began to use *America* as well, and before long it had stuck.

Three More Possible Origins for *America*

★ ★ ★ ★ ★ ★ ★ ★ ★ ★ ★ ★

1. European explorers may have picked up the name *Amerrique*—"Land of the Wind" in Mayan—from South American natives.

2. The name could have come from a British customs officer named Richard Ameryk, who sponsored John Cabot's voyage to Newfoundland in 1497 and possibly some pre-Columbian explorations of the continent.

3. Another theory claims that early Norse explorers called the mysterious new land *Ommerike,* meaning "farthest outland."

Q. What was the first English colony established in North America?

A. Roanoke Island (Jamestown was the first *permanent* colony). Roanoke Island, Virginia (in modern-day North Carolina), was settled in 1587 under the command of John White. This colony got off to a good start, and a child was born to White's daughter—Virginia Dare, the first child born to English parents on now-American soil. In August 1587 White left the burgeoning colony for England. A war with Spain delayed White's return, but when he again landed at Roanoke in 1590, he found nothing. The colony had been completely abandoned—nothing remained, not a shred of clothing, not a pot or pan, and not a single person. Structures had been carefully dismantled. There was only one cryptic clue: the word *Croatoan* etched into a fence post. To this day the fate of the colonists remains unknown.

Q. Who was likely the first European to lay eyes on Alabama?

A. Spanish explorer Alonso Álvarez de Pineda. He was searching for a passage from the Gulf of Mexico to the

Pacific Ocean. He didn't find one, obviously, but instead mapped much of the western shore of the gulf. During his expedition in 1519, he sailed into Mobile Bay.

Q. Who was the first European explorer to sail into New York Harbor?

A. Giovanni da Verrazzano. Sailing for France, da Verrazzano was doing a quick survey of the North American East Coast in 1524. Initially landing off North Carolina, he followed the coast north to see what he could find. Unfortunately, he seems to have been moving too quickly, causing him to miss a number of details, such as Chesapeake Bay. He also misunderstood some of what he saw, such as mistaking the Hudson River for an inland lake. He named the modern New York City area *Nouvelle-Angoulême*, a name that, of course, failed to stick.

> ★★★ **FAST FACT** ★★★
> The Verrazano-Narrows Bridge in New York, which connects Brooklyn and Staten Island, was named in honor of the explorer. Unfortunately, it misspells *da Verrazzano*.

TRUE OR FALSE Spanish explorer Juan Ponce de León was searching for the fabled fountain of youth when he discovered Florida instead.

ANSWER Most likely false. Although this search has become legend, Ponce de León did not become linked to the fountain until after his death in 1521. The first published reference associating the explorer with the fountain of youth was in 1535 in the *Historia General y Natural de las Indias* by Gonzalo

Ten Spanish Explorers

★ ★ ★ ★ ★ ★ ★ ★ ★ ★ ★ ★

1. Juan Ponce de León (1460-1521) colonized Puerto Rico and led the first European expedition to Florida.

2. Alonso Álvarez de Pineda (1494-1520) sailed along the southern Gulf Coast, entered the mouth of the Mississippi River, and mapped the coast of Texas. He made the first European landing at the mouth of the Rio Grande.

3. Lucas Vasquez de Ayllon (ca. 1475-1526) was a colonial judge who established a settlement in South Carolina in 1526.

4. Pánfilo de Narváez (ca. 1478-1528) led an expedition of inland Florida in 1528. He was plagued by desertion, hurricanes, lost supplies, and hostile encounters with natives. He did not survive.

5. Álvar Núñez Cabeza de Vaca (ca. 1490-1560) survived Pánfilo de Narváez's disastrous expedition and led three other survivors on an eight-year odyssey by land and sea across the American Southeast and back to Mexico.

6. Hernando de Soto (ca. 1496/97-1542) led an expedition across southeastern North America. He was the first European to see the inland Mississippi River.

7. Juan Rodríguez Cabrillo (?-1543), who himself was Portuguese, was involved in the Spanish conquest of Central America and went on to explore and claim the California region for Spain.

8. Francisco Vásquez de Coronado (ca. 1510-54) explored the American Southwest in search of a fabled city of gold. He was the first European to encounter the Pueblo people and to see the Grand Canyon.

9. Pedro Menéndez de Avilés (1519-74) established a Spanish settlement in St. Augustine, Florida. It became the oldest continuously inhabited city in North America.

10. Juan de Oñate (ca. 1550-1630) led the exploration of New Mexico. In 1601 he sent an exploring party into present-day Kansas.

Fernandez de Oviedo, who cited the explorer's search for a fountain of restorative water to cure his impotence. The believability of this account is questionable, however, as Ponce de León didn't even mention the fountain in his travel notes and had already sired children at the time of his 1513 voyage.

⭐ The United States was very possibly the first nation ever to grow out of a business venture. The men who sailed into Chesapeake Bay in 1607 and built the Jamestown settlement worked for the Virginia Company of London, a joint-stock company that sold shares to gentlemen and merchants and used the proceeds to fund colonization. But business was bad—the Jamestown settlement was a disaster, trying and failing to turn a significant profit for more than a decade and a half. Finally, in 1624, King James I dissolved the bankrupt company and made Virginia a crown colony.

Q. How did Virginia get its name?

A. As the first English colony in the New World, it was named after the reigning English monarch, Elizabeth I. Because she never married, she was known as "The Virgin Queen," and *Virginia* is a reference to that fact.

Q. Where was John Rolfe married, and who was his famous bride?

A. John Rolfe married Pocahontas in the colony of Jamestown in 1614. Pocahontas was the daughter of Chief Powhatan, leader of the Powhatan nations. Although relations between Jamestown and the Powhatan nations had often been violent, this marriage brought eight years of peace between the two groups.

Q. Every schoolchild knows that the Pilgrims landed at Plymouth Rock in modern-day Massachusetts in 1620. But where had they intended to go?

A. The mouth of the Hudson River, near present-day New York City. At that time, it was in the northern part of the English colony of Virginia, and the English government had issued them a patent of land. They had gone off course during the voyage of the *Mayflower*.

★ The pilgrims named Plymouth, Massachusetts, after the port of England from which they had sailed. The spot where these travelers first touched land in the New World is marked traditionally by Plymouth Rock.

TRUE OR FALSE When the Pilgrims arrived at Plymouth in 1620, they established a type of communist economy.

ANSWER True. More than 200 years before Karl Marx wrote *The Communist Manifesto*, the Pilgrims of Plymouth Bay Colony adopted ideas of communal ownership and agricultural production. To their disappointment, however, they discovered that people were not willing to work hard enough for the common good. When every family was responsible for raising its own agriculture, the amount of production increased dramatically.

Q. Where in the Pacific were the Sandwich Islands?

A. In Hawaii. This is an old name for the Hawaiian Islands. In 1778 British sea captain James Cook "discovered" them and named them for his good friend John Montague, the Earl of Sandwich.

Q. Did Peter Minuit really buy Manhattan Island for the Dutch for 24 dollars?

A. Essentially he did. On May 24, 1626, he traded goods worth 60 Dutch guilders to Native Americans for the island. In the 19th century, that amount was calculated to be equal to 24 dollars. To bring some perspective to the transaction, however, an average Dutch soldier in 1626 would have made about 10 guilders a month.

Q. In 1636 Roger Williams left Massachusetts Bay Colony and went elsewhere. Why did he depart, and where did he go?

A. Williams was a theologian who advocated tolerance and free thinking, neither of which had any place in Massachusetts, so he was asked to leave. Traveling west from Plymouth, he founded his own settlement beside Narragansett Bay, naming it Providence in the belief that divine intervention had led him there. In 1644 he secured a land patent from England, establishing the beginnings of Rhode Island.

TRUE OR FALSE William Penn established Pennsylvania to be a Quaker colony.

ANSWER False. Although Penn was a Quaker himself, he welcomed followers of a variety of faiths and from a number of different countries into the colony he chartered in 1681, making it a true refuge for religious tolerance.

★★★ **FAST FACT** ★★★

Pennsylvania—meaning "forests of Penn"—was not named for William Penn. Instead, King Charles II suggested the name for Penn's father, Admiral Sir William Penn.

Q. King Philip's War may have been early America's worst conflict. Where was it fought?

A. In Massachusetts and Rhode Island. King Philip was also known as Metacom, and he was the son of Massasoit, the Wampanoag leader who had saved the original Plymouth colony by helping the Pilgrims establish themselves and teaching them to farm in the New World. By 1675 the population of English colonists in New England had grown to about 52,000, and Metacom feared that colonists would force the Wampanoag off their traditional lands.

Relations between Native Americans and English colonists became more and more tense, and after deadly provocations on both sides, Metacom began raiding English villages. For 14 months in 1675 and '76, both sides set modern Massachusetts and Rhode Island aflame, destroying towns, villages, and property. In August 1676, however, Plymouth militia and Native American allies tracked down Metacom at Mount Hope, Rhode Island, where they beheaded, drew, and quartered him, to end the hostilities.

TRUE OR FALSE The English established Georgia as a penal colony.

ANSWER False. James Oglethorpe was a social reformer who was particularly concerned about people forced into prison because of debt. He sought a charter for a new colony where the "worthy poor" might have a chance to improve their lives. King George II granted the charter in 1732, a full 50 years after the previous North American colony had been established. As it turned out, however, no prisoners or debtors sentenced to prison were among those who joined Oglethorpe in establishing the first colonial settlement—what has come to be Savannah—the next year.

Q. Where was the War of Jenkins' Ear?

A. Along the border between Georgia and Florida. The Spanish were well established in Florida before the English colonized Georgia, and tension between the two countries in the area had been thick for some time. The war got its name from an incident in 1731, a year before Georgia was chartered: English Captain Robert Jenkins was accused of piracy by a Spanish officer who then lopped off his ear. The situation didn't heat up until 1740, however, when James Oglethorpe invaded Spanish Florida. He couldn't hold his territory and retreated back to Georgia, where his forces held off Spanish invasion in 1742. In the end, little was gained or lost between the two colonies.

Q. Which of the 13 colonies was founded by fishermen?

A. New Hampshire, which, ironically, has just 18 miles of shore-line, the least amount of any coastal colony or state—then or now. David Thompson and his partners were given a British land grant on November 15, 1622, and they settled at the mouth of the Piscataqua River, at the place that today is called Odiorne's Point in Rye. Thompson named the settlement Pannaway Plantation, and its purpose was entirely commercial—it was intended to survive through fishing and fur trapping.

SCIENCE AND NATURE

★ ★ ★ ★ ★ ★ ★ ★ ★ ★ ★ ★

Each of us is certainly a product of the world around us,
yet that world can have two sides. America has always
been a nation of innovations and inventors, which has
helped the nation move forward. But the natural world
sometimes reminds us of the power it has at its disposal.
These pieces of trivia range from the most positive
scientific advances to the worst natural disasters.

Q. What place gave inventor Thomas Edison his nickname?

A. Menlo Park, New Jersey. Thomas Alva
Edison, perhaps the most influential
inventor America has ever seen, lived and
worked there for only six years at the beginning of his career, but those years were productive enough to earn him the nickname
"The Wizard of Menlo Park." During
his time there, Edison patented about
400 inventions, including the phonograph.
Some of these inventions were also used to
refine and perfect the incandescent electric lightbulb.

Q. Two bicycle-shop owners from Dayton, Ohio, did something
significant in North Carolina. What was it?

A. Wilbur and Orville Wright achieved the first machine-
powered flight. Based in Kitty Hawk and Kill Devil Hills,
the brothers experimented with gliders for nearly four years until,

on December 17, 1903, Orville climbed into a motor-powered glider and made his 12-second flight.

★ San Francisco was awoken by an earthquake at about 5:12 in the morning on April 18, 1906. Estimated anywhere between 7.7 and 8.3 on the Richter scale (which had not yet been developed), the quake lasted for 45 seconds, toppling buildings and destroying roads and bridges. Even more damaging, the quake ruptured gas mains throughout the city, causing enormous fires that burned out of control for days at a time. Between the powerful quake and the resulting fires, nearly 90 percent of San Francisco was destroyed, with almost 3,000 people dead and 225,000 homeless. The damage was estimated at some $400 million (more than $8.2 billion in today's dollars).

> ★★★ **FAST FACT** ★★★
>
> **Helium was discovered at the University of Kansas in 1905.**

Q. What technological marvel was introduced at the World's Columbian Exposition, held in Chicago in 1893?

A. The Ferris wheel. Organizers had wanted a feat to rival the Eiffel Tower, which debuted at a world's fair in Paris four years earlier.

Q. What are the two most active volcanoes in Hawaii?

A. Kilauea and Mauna Loa. And not just Hawaii—they are two of the most active volcanoes in the world. Mauna Loa is also notable for being one of the world's tallest mountains; measured from its base at the bottom of the Pacific Ocean, it would actually be taller than Mount Everest.

In 1946 John Mauchly and J. Presper Eckert completed development of the first general-purpose digital computer, the Electronic Numerical Integrator And Computer (ENIAC), at the University of Pennsylvania. The ENIAC could perform complicated equations some 50,000 times faster than a human being. It weighed 27 tons, occupied 680 square feet, and gulped 150 kilowatts of juice. (It is a myth, however, that its power draw dimmed the lights in Philadelphia.)

Q. Where did Hurricane Katrina make landfall on August 28, 2005?

A. The coast of Mississippi. The storm was headed for New Orleans, where it hit the next day. There were doubts about the strength of the levees around New Orleans, built to protect the city from just such threats, and as some predicted, the levees failed almost immediately, causing massive flooding throughout the city. By the time the storm had subsided, nearly 2,000 peo-

The Worst Earthquake Sequence in the Continental United States

* * * * * * * * * * * *

A series of about 200 quakes—three of them believed to have been between 7 and 8 on the modern Richter scale, and seven believed to be more than 6—struck near New Madrid, Missouri, in a period of less than two months in 1811 and 1812. The first quake in this series occurred early in the morning of December 16, 1811, its intensity estimated to have been 7.7. It caused parts of the Mississippi River to flow backward and was felt in New York City, Washington, D.C., and Charleston, South Carolina. The ground near the Mississippi River rose and fell, cracks opened in the earth, and trees were bent and broken. The last major quake in this sequence, reported to have been as bad as or worse than the first, hit at 3:45 A.M. on February 7, 1812.

ple had died and more than $80 billion in damage had been wrought. Furthermore, nearly half a million people had been displaced from New Orleans.

Q. Physicist Enrico Fermi and his team worked at Clinton Labs in the Smoky Mountains during World War II to help develop the atomic bomb. What happened to this facility after the war?

A. It was renamed the Oak Ridge National Laboratory, and its research focus shifted away from nuclear weaponry and toward other research initiatives, particularly in the field of nuclear energy and nuclear medicine. As a matter of fact, Oak Ridge became one of the first centers for creating isotopes used in cancer treatment.

Q. In 1979 a nuclear accident introduced the word *meltdown* to a large section of the American public. Where did this accident occur?

A. Three Mile Island, Pennsylvania. As a result of mechanical failure, poor instrument design, and human error, the reactor's core temperature reached 4,300 degrees Fahrenheit in a matter of hours. Scientists feared that a hydrogen bubble near the core could explode and breach the core's containment with devastating consequences. Finally, it was determined that the hydrogen was not a threat and that the  core had stabilized. Although, in the end, little damage had been done, fear of what could have happened dampened public enthusiasm for nuclear energy.

Q. A combination of archaic farming techniques in the Great Plains and one of the worst droughts in American history produced what natural disaster in the 1930s?

A. The Dust Bowl. With no crops or prairie grasses to hold down depleted topsoil, high winds endemic to the area whipped dried dirt and soil into the air—in 1935 alone officials estimated that some 850 million tons of topsoil had been blown off the land. At times the dust storms were so bad that visibility was limited to just a few feet; the worst of them traveled eastward, causing the sky to darken as far east as Washington, D.C. On April 14, 1935, a day known as "Black Sunday," there were over 20 massive dust storms throughout the plains, blotting out the sun and turning day into night.

TRUE OR FALSE The Smithsonian Institution is the world's largest museum and research institution.

ANSWER True. The Smithsonian houses over 137 million artifacts in its 19 museums and world-famous zoo, the majority of which are located in Washington, D.C., including 11 clustered on the National Mall. The Smithsonian's collections are impressive, but what makes the institution so special is the network of scientists and scholars working under the Smithsonian's auspices. Each year millions of dollars are spent on research projects that range from cures for avian flu to analysis of acid rain and on funding research centers around the Americas.

★★★ **FAST FACT** ★★★

When the Smithsonian curators inventoried their holdings in 1982, they found among the stockpile 100,000 bats, 2,300 spark plugs, 14,300 sea sponges, 2,587 musical instruments, and 10 specimens of dinosaur excrement.

Q. What river that feeds the Great Lakes is infamous for catching on fire?

A. The Cuyahoga River in Cleveland. Between 1868 and '87 the river caught fire three times, and in 1912 an oil slick floating atop the water ignited, causing a massive explosion and fire that killed five people. In 1936 an inferno raged for five days before being put out. In 1941, and again in 1948, the Cuyahoga went up in flames to little notice. The worst river fire to date was in 1952. The five-alarm blaze sent flames high into the air and caused more than $1 million in damage. The most recent fire was in 1969.

> *"The fire was a bad thing, sure, but some good came out of it in the end. Many people see this fire as being a catalyst for the federal Clean Water Act and other environmental laws."*
> —Jane Goodman, Cleveland-area councilwoman

Q. It's the most famous earthquake fault in the country, running 800 miles along the length of California. Can you name it?

A. The San Andreas Fault. First identified in 1895, it marks the boundary between the Pacific and North American plates. The San Andreas Fault is so large that geologists talk about its different parts as distinct entities, each with its own behavior.

Q. What natural disaster hit the Mississippi River in the spring of 1927?

A. Swollen with massive rains that had actually begun the previous fall, the Mississippi River broke through its levees and flooded—a region the combined size of Massachusetts, Connecticut, Vermont, and New Hampshire was under water, and at one point the river was nearly 70 miles wide. When all was said and done, some 700,000 people were displaced, with nearly half a billion dollars worth of damage caused in Illinois, Iowa, Mississippi, Missouri, Tennessee, and Louisiana.

⎯⎯⎯⎯⎯⎯⎯⎯⎯⎯⎯⎯⎯⎯⎯⎯⎯⎯⎯

★ The Salk Institute for Biological Studies is located in La Jolla, part of San Diego, California. But that's not where Dr. Jonas Salk developed his polio vaccine. His research in the 1940s and '50s was performed at the University of Pittsburgh, where Salk was on staff. The vaccine, proven safe and effective, was announced to the world on April 12, 1955. Salk turned to Southern California as a home to his research institute in 1960.

⎯⎯⎯⎯⎯⎯⎯⎯⎯⎯⎯⎯⎯⎯⎯⎯⎯⎯⎯

Q. The summer of 1910 saw the Big Burn, a wildfire that reshaped fire management policies in the United States. Where did this fire take place?

A. In Idaho and Montana. Drought conditions stretched throughout the West that year, and by August, numerous small wildfires had begun to burn. On August 20 a cold front swept in, sending powerful winds howling through the region. The small wildfires suddenly kicked up, racing across parched mountains and fields and joining forces with one another. Within a day the conflagration was a wall of flame that stretched an estimated 185 miles long and 65 miles wide. And just as quickly as the blaze began, it ended. On the evening of August 21, a steady rain began pouring, putting out the fires. In just two days, more than 3 million acres (an area the size of Connecticut) had burned, completely obliterating several towns and killing about 85 people.

Q. This interdisciplinary research facility at the University of Illinois houses some of the most advanced computer and intelligence projects in the United States. What is it?

A. The Beckman Institute. Completed in 1989 with a $40-million gift from engineer Arthur Beckman, the Beckman Institute is home to more than 600 researchers, divided into 13 distinct research groups. Projects and research teams are organized around four major themes: biological intelligence, integrative imaging, molecular and electronic nanostructures, and human-computer intelligent interaction. The institute is most famous for its artificial intelligence research in the area of human-computer intelligent interaction. One of the more intriguing projects is computer face recognition, providing computers with the ability to identify human faces by "sight."

Q. Where did the deadliest hurricane in U.S. history hit?

A. Galveston, Texas, in September 1900. Climatologists dismissed the notion that a hurricane could devastate the island city of Galveston, but they were wrong. Unfortunately, the initial cavalier attitude toward hurricanes may have played a part in the huge loss of life—between 8,000 and 12,000 deaths—because less than half the population evacuated and some people came from Houston just to watch. The U.S. Weather Bureau ranked the storm a category 4 hurricane with wind speeds measured at 100 miles per hour before the measuring device blew away. Other records say winds peaked around 145 miles per hour. The hurricane wiped out about three-quarters of the city and caused nearly $20 million in damage.

★★★ **FAST FACT** ★★★
San Francisco was home to the first all-electronic TV, invented by Philo T. Farnsworth in 1927.

Q. Considered dormant since its previous eruption in the 1850s, what volcano in the Pacific Northwest came back to life in the 1980s?

A. Mount St. Helens. On May 18, 1980, the volcano, located in Washington State, exploded with the most powerful and destructive eruption in U.S. history. A 12-mile-high plume of ash and rock spewed into the sky, sending molten rock across the area at speeds of more than 600 miles per hour. Over the next nine hours the eruption continued

unabated, sending 540 million tons of ash skyward, where it drifted across the continent, settling as far away as New England. The eruption's statistics are staggering: 57 people killed, with scores more injured. Every nearby structure was completely buried. Hundreds of miles of highways and railroads were destroyed, and animal and plant life was annihilated for miles around.

★ The forerunner of the Internet was ARPANET, which began to build computer networks in the 1960s. The first two computers to be linked were at UCLA and Stanford Research Institute, and the first message (which was incomplete because the system crashed while it was being sent) was on October 29, 1969. By December 5, 1969, the network had grown to four locations, with the University of California at Santa Barbara and the University of Utah joining in.

Q. What disastrous event that took place in Chicago in 1871 was blamed on a cow?

A. The Great Chicago Fire. It began in or near a southside barn at about 9:00 P.M. on Sunday, October 8, 1871. Thanks to a series of alarm relay and communication errors, fatigued firefighters (who had battled a major fire the day before) didn't show up until 10:00 or later, by which time the inferno had engulfed several blocks. Before midnight it had leaped the Chicago River and spread into the Loop. The Gasworks blew up around midnight. As Monday dawned, the wind-flogged flames headed north at several blocks per hour. Much of the city had been built of wood. Rain fell Monday night, and firefighters finally halted the spread in Tuesday morning's wee hours. The Great Chicago Fire had consumed 17,450 buildings, 73 miles of streets, and 300 lives.

> ★ ★ ★ **FAST FACT** ★ ★ ★
>
> The largest silver nugget was found just outside of Aspen, Colorado. Prospected from the Smuggler Mine in 1894, this nugget weighed 1,840 pounds!

Q. The United States—including Alaska and Hawaii—has experienced a number of earthquakes over the years, but which was the biggest?

A. The most powerful tremor in U.S. history—lasting three minutes and measuring 9.2 on the Richter scale—struck Prince William Sound in Alaska on March 28, 1964. Only 15 people died in the quake itself, but the resulting tsunami, which reached more than 200 feet high at Valdez Inlet, killed 110 more people and caused $311 million in property damage. The city of Anchorage was hit particularly hard, with 30 downtown blocks suffering heavy damage.

POP CULTURE

★ ★ ★ ★ ★ ★ ★ ★ ★ ★ ★

All those things that seem vitally important at the moment but become more and more difficult to remember as time goes on make up our pop culture. The fads and fun that influenced the American way of life take us back to the first time we experienced them. Nostalgia lives—all we need to do is remember.

Q. From where does German chocolate cake get its name?

A. From one of its main ingredients, Baker's German's Sweet Chocolate. (You knew the answer couldn't be Germany in a book like this!) Baker's Chocolate was a company founded in Massachusetts in 1780. Baker's German's Sweet Chocolate was named for Samuel German, an employee who developed the chocolate in 1852.

Q. Why is the White House white?

A. Initially, the building known as the White House was actually gray. It was painted white after the War of 1812 to cover smoke stains sustained when the building was burned by British troops.

Q. What animal that went on to become a national symbol was found after a New Mexico forest fire?

A. Smokey Bear. The black bear cub was found burned and clinging to the branch of a scorched pine tree in 1950, and it soon won the hearts of the American public. The Forest Service had started a fire prevention program a few years before this that starred a cartoon bear named Smokey. When they heard about the burned bear cub, they knew they'd found their real-life Smokey.

Q. What famous Hollywood eatery was home to the Cobb Salad?

A. The Brown Derby. True to its name, the Brown Derby was actually shaped like a derby hat, complete with brim. The salad is named after the restaurant's owner, Robert Cobb, who, so the story goes, was wandering through the kitchen one night grabbing ingredients for something to eat. His combination of lettuce, avocado, chicken, bacon, boiled eggs, and more became so immediately popular that it was added to the menu.

★★★ **FAST FACT** ★★★

The first automatic telephone exchange capable of transmitting messages 24 hours a day was established in 1892 in the town of La Porte, Indiana.

In 1899, an era when most cops rode horses, Akron, Ohio, became the first U.S. city to operate a police car. The battery-operated patrol wagon cost $2,400. It was equipped with electric lights, gongs, and a stretcher and could go 16 miles per hour (and travel 30 miles between charges). The police cruiser's first driver was Officer Louis Mueller Sr., whose inaugural assignment was to pick up a drunk person making trouble at Main and Exchange Streets.

Q. What is the name of the historic development on New York's Long Island that, in many ways, set the tone for American suburbia in the 1950s?

A. Levittown. In 1949 William J. Levitt bought a 1,500-acre potato field with the intention of building block after block of quiet homes, running along quiet side streets. For just under $10,000, post–World War II Americans could get their own little four-room place—landscaped and filled with appliances. Levitt repeated his suburban success on eight square miles in Pennsylvania, building a densely populated town of 70,000.

Q. What mood-lifting dairy product came from Youngstown, Ohio?

A. Good Humor bars. In 1920, ice cream–shop owner Harry Burt inserted wooden sticks into ice cream bars, creating "the new, clean, convenient way to eat ice cream." He named his product according to the popular belief that one's palate affects one's mood and sold them through a fleet of shiny white trucks, each stocked with a friendly Good Humor Man and all the ice cream bars kids could eat.

Q. Where was the first American radio station?

A. The first U.S. broadcast by a radio station took place from KDKA in East Pittsburgh, Pennsylvania, on November 2, 1920. It announced that Warren Harding had been elected president.

Q. Where did a steel coil become a popular children's toy?

A. Philadelphia. Richard James was a naval engineer who, in 1943, accidentally knocked a torsion spring off his desk. Watching it bounce around his office, he saw the potential for a toy and developed a steel formula that would allow the spring to walk down stairs. James's wife, Betty, came up with the name *Slinky*, the Swedish word for "stealthy, sleek, and sinuous."

Q. How did the bikini swimsuit get its name?

A. Before there was a skimpy bathing suit, there was Bikini Atoll in the Marshall Islands of the South Pacific. On July 1, 1946, this was the site of a highly publicized U.S. nuclear bomb detonation test. The bikini swimsuit, which debuted later that month, was named for that test—designer Louis Réard hoped his swimsuit would make a similar explosion in the fashion world.

Cracker Jack was invented in 1896, when enterprising Chicago-based candy maker Louis Rueckheim figured out a way to keep molasses-covered popcorn from sticking together. Though instantly popular, the childhood treat became an icon of American culture when it was mentioned in the 1908 song "Take Me Out to the Ballgame." Its longevity was

Saratoga Chips?
★ ★ ★ ★ ★ ★ ★ ★ ★ ★ ★

If you can't eat just one potato chip, blame it on chef George Crum, who reportedly created the salty snack in 1853 at Moon's Lake House near Saratoga Springs, New York. Fed up with a customer who continuously complained that his fried potatoes weren't crunchy enough, Crum sliced the potatoes as thin as possible, fried them in hot grease, and doused them with salt. The customer loved them, and "Saratoga Chips" quickly became a popular item at the lodge and throughout New England.

secured in 1912, when the company came up with the brilliant marketing idea of including a prize in every box.

Q. How long have they been rolling Easter eggs at the White House?

A. Since 1878. In that year, President Rutherford B. Hayes introduced the first White House Easter Egg Roll.

Q. When did the White House officially get its name?

A. Not until 1901 under President Theodore Roosevelt. Before then the presidential domicile was sometimes called the "President's Palace," the "President's House," or the "Executive Mansion."

"I don't know whether it's the finest public housing in America or the crown jewel of the prison system."
—President Bill Clinton on the White House

Q. On August 14, 1945, World War II was finally over. One photograph, of a sailor who impulsively grabbed a nurse and kissed her, has come to exemplify the excitement felt across the country. Where was this photo taken?

A. New York's Times Square. *Life* magazine photographer Alfred Eisenstaedt spotted a sailor running about, kissing young and old women alike. As the

★ ★ ★ **FAST FACT** ★ ★ ★
Seattle's Space Needle was built for the 1962 World's Fair.

sailor grabbed the nurse and kissed her, Eisenstaedt clicked the shutter. Many people have since claimed to be the subjects in the photo. Eisenstaedt identified the nurse as Edith Shain.

Q. The restaurant in this landmark Boston hotel saw the creation of the Boston cream pie and a kind of roll that carries the hotel's name. What is it?

A. The Parker House. Opened by Harvey Parker in 1855, it has remained in business ever since, becoming the nation's longest-lived continuously operating hotel. Boston cream pie and Parker House rolls are only part of the heritage of this establishment.

Q. In 1912 the Japanese ambassador to the United States presented the nation with a gift. What was it?

A. Three thousand flowering cherry trees. These were planted in Washington, D.C., where an annual Cherry Blossom Festival has been celebrated each spring since 1935 (with a brief suspension during World War II). A second gift of 3,800 cherry trees was given to the United States by Japan in 1965. These were planted near the Washington Monument.

★ ★ ★ **FAST FACT** ★ ★ ★

The 1904 World's Fair in St. Louis, Missouri, marked the debut of iced tea.

Q. Where did the first typhoid fever outbreak traced to Typhoid Mary occur?

A. In Oyster Bay, New York, on Long Island in 1906. Investigators discovered that Mary Mallon had worked as a cook in a home there. On investigation of Mallon's employment records, it was discovered that typhoid fever had been following her from job to job. Mallon was found—still working as a cook—in New York City in 1907. Doctors examined Mallon and determined that she was immune to typhoid fever but that she carried the bacteria that caused it, possibly in an infected gallbladder. She remained in quarantine until 1910, but after that she still seemed to be spreading the disease. By the time she was found and quarantined again in 1915, it was believed that she had spread typhoid fever to 51 people, three of whom had fatal cases.

Q. What city inspired the names of the properties in the Monopoly board game?

A. Atlantic City, New Jersey. Although the origins of the game have been disputed in court, in 1934 Charles Darrow, an out-of-work salesman, sold the game featuring Atlantic City street names to Parker Brothers. One error was never corrected, however. Marven Gardens, an area just south of Atlantic City, was misspelled *Marvin Gardens* and remains in the game to this day.

Q. Where did corn flakes come from?

A. Battle Creek, Michigan. That's where Dr. J. H. Kellogg ran what he called a *sanitarium*, dedicated to healthy living. He and his brother, W. K. Kellogg, were interested in finding new foods to support that goal. Completely by accident in 1894, the brothers discovered a way to create toasted wheat flakes, and they started experimenting with other grains. The corn variety became quite popular, and the broth-ers started to sell it commercially. They fought over the recipe— W. K. wanted to add sugar, while J. H. wanted the cereal to remain pure and be sold as a health food. Ultimately W. K. started his own company, Kellogg's, which today is known to breakfast lovers nationwide.

An Unexpected Fireball

★ ★ ★ ★ ★ ★ ★ ★ ★ ★ ★ ★

At the East Ohio Gas Company in Cleveland, Ohio, on the afternoon of October 20, 1944, a leak developed in a storage tank holding more than 650 million gallons of liquefied natural gas. The winds blowing off Lake Erie pushed the white vapor into the sewer system, where the gas mixed with air and became explosive. The resulting blast created a fireball towering over half a mile high—it was visible more than seven miles away. Jets of flame blasted out of the sewer, propelling manhole covers into the air. The explosion set into motion a chain of events that resulted in 130 deaths and left 700 people homeless.

Q. What unhygienic act led two researchers at Johns Hopkins University to invent saccharin?

A. Constantine Fahlberg, a researcher working in the laboratory of professor Ira Remsen, spilled a chemical on his hands one day in 1879 and didn't bother to wash them before lunch. Unexpectedly, the bread he ate tasted unusually sweet. In 1880 the two scientists jointly published this discovery, and in 1884 Fahlberg obtained a patent and began mass-producing saccharin without Remsen. The use of saccharin didn't become widespread until sugar was rationed during World War I. Its popularity increased even further during the 1960s and '70s with the manufacture of Sweet'N Low and diet soft drinks.

Q. What did Manhattanites do with garbage before big scows existed to remove it?

A. They threw it in the water to make new land. A good

★★★ **FAST FACT** ★★★

The first speed limit in the United States was set in 1901 in Connecticut, at 12 mph.

percentage of the Manhattan coast is built on garbage or *landfill*, as it's more politely called.

Q. Where was the first U.S. auto accident?

A. So far as is known, the first car wreck in history occurred in Ohio City, Ohio, in 1891, when local resident John Lambert—who designed and built his own automobile—lost control of his ride and smashed into a hitching post.

TRUE OR FALSE A military base was partially responsible for the McDonald's drive-through window.

ANSWER True. At Fort Huachuca in Sierra Vista, Arizona, uniformed soldiers were prohibited from entering civilian places of business, but sometimes they got hungry. Base commanders asked a nearby McDonald's restaurant to install a window where soldiers could be served without going in. The fast-food eatery was happy to do so—its first drive-through customer was served on January 24, 1975. The where and when of the first drive-through window from any restaurant is more difficult to pin down. That claim has been made by Red's Giant Hamburg in Springfield, Missouri; Maid-Rite in Springfield, Illinois; In-N-Out Burger in Baldwin Park, California; and Jack in the Box in San Diego. Each of these opened their windows in the late 1940s or early 1950s.

Q. Where was ranch dressing developed?

A. Believe it or not, it actually started out on a ranch—a dude ranch in Santa Barbara, California. Opened in 1954 by Steve and Gayle Henson, the Hidden Valley Ranch served a special buttermilk-based house dressing that was so popular that visitors came just to buy it.

THE NATION'S FOUNDING

★ ★ ★ ★ ★ ★ ★ ★ ★ ★ ★ ★

It is the defining moment in American history—the Revolution. A number of locations during the colonial period and the time during and after the war itself have become iconic in their importance for the United States. How many of them do you know?

Q. Most historians mark April 19, 1775, as the start of the American Revolution, when the "shot heard round the world" was fired. Where was that shot fired?

A. Lexington, Massachusetts. British troops, 700 strong, were advancing on Concord to destroy arms and munitions belonging to the patriots. At Lexington they found 77 members of the local militia known as "Minutemen." Someone—to this day no one knows who—fired an unordered shot. The gunfire that followed resulted in eight Americans killed and eight wounded.

Q. On March 5, 1770, an angry mob began to collect at the Custom House in Boston, Massachusetts. What historical event took place next?

A. The Boston Massacre. The confrontation started with curses and taunts against the soldiers and escalated into a barrage of snowballs and junk. Soon the mob was egging on the troops to fire. When Redcoat reinforcements arrived, their cap-

tain tried to calm down the situation, but someone (probably an angry Loyalist) behind the British line encouraged the soldiers to open fire. Just then, something—many accounts say it was a stick or hunk of wood—knocked a soldier down. He stood up and fired, and a ragged volley followed before the captain could stop it. The toll was three colonials dead, with two more dying from their injuries the next day, and half a dozen or so wounded.

Q. This Puritan town in New England is known for the unusual accusations and trials that were held there in 1692. Can you identify it?

A. Salem, Massachusetts. Betty Parris and Abigail Williams started behaving strangely—throwing things, crawling under tables, crying, shaking, and complaining of being pricked by pins (behavior most modern parents would identify as a tantrum). They claimed they were being tormented by the specters of three outcast women from the town: the homeless Sarah Good, the immoral Sarah Osborne, and the Caribbean slave Tituba. All three were immediately arrested. Over the next year the two girls, along with several other town children, accused dozens more townspeople of witchcraft. The accused were tried in a specially commissioned court by witchcraft "experts" and almost universally sentenced to death by hanging. By the time the governor of the colony put an end to the madness, 25 or more innocent people had died—19 by hanging.

⭐ At the beginning of the American Revolution, roughly 2.5 million people lived in the 13 original colonies. The colonies' population, only about 250,000 in 1700, had exploded in the years before the Revolution. But not all of these colonists had come from England. The colonies of New England were predominantly of English descent, but inhabitants of the mid-Atlantic and Southern colonies were made up primarily of German, Scottish, and Irish immigrants.

TRUE OR FALSE On May 10, 1775, a meeting of leaders from each of the 13 colonies convened in Philadelphia, Pennsylvania, at Independence Hall.

ANSWER False. Although it has since been renamed Independence Hall, the building was known as the Pennsylvania State House at the time. This meeting was the Second Continental Congress, which in the next two years would appoint George Washington commander-in-chief of revolutionary forces and approve the Declaration of Independence. In 1777 the Congress was forced to leave Independence Hall when the British army occupied Philadelphia, but after the war the body again took up residence there.

Q. Which colony sponsored the largest number of signers of the Declaration of Independence?

A. Pennsylvania. The Second Continental Congress, which commissioned the declaration, included representatives from each of the 13 colonies, and 56 delegates signed the document. Pennsylvania sent nine signers, including Benjamin Franklin.

Monticello, Thomas Jefferson's home in Virginia, is a showplace of Jefferson's obsession with invention. During his time there the house featured, among other new ideas, automatic doors, a revolving bookstand, a primitive copy machine, and the modern dumbwaiter. But Jefferson's most famous invention was the Great Clock, an ingenious device that kept track of both the day and the time; it also struck an enormous gong on the roof of the main house hourly.

Q. Led by Ethan Allen, one band of Revolutionary War soldiers called themselves the Green Mountain Boys. Where are the Green Mountains?

A. Vermont. Land speculators such as Ethan Allen and his brothers organized armed groups and used intimidation and violence to keep the area out of the control of the New York colony. All ready to fight by the time the colonies sought independence from Britain, the Green Mountain Boys achieved the colonies' first war victory, capturing Fort Ticonderoga on May 10, 1775. (Although, truth be told, that "victory" mostly consisted of walking through the gates and taking over while the British slept.)

> ★★★ **FAST FACT** ★★★
> Thomas Jefferson, of course, appears on the nickel. On the back of that coin is Monticello. In addition, Monticello also appears on the backside of certain $2 bills.

Q. Benedict Arnold's name is synonymous with treason, and rightfully so. But what specifically did he intend to betray?

A. He offered to surrender the fort at West Point, New York, to the British for £20,000 in 1780, the year he was put in command of this fort. Arnold had been a friend of George Washington, a successful businessman, and a hero of the Revolutionary War, but too many setbacks had made him frustrated. Although Arnold's plot was stopped, Arnold himself eluded capture, and he became a brigadier general in the British Army. After the war, he and his family lived in England and in Canada.

Q. How did an unfinished fort in Charleston Harbor hold off a British invasion in 1776?

A. The unfinished and unnamed fort provided an intriguing target for a British fleet on June 28, 1776. Built from soft, spongy palmetto wood and reinforced with sand, the fort withstood fire from the British ships. It was reported that some of the cannonballs got stuck in the wood or even bounced off. After taking damaging fire from inside the fort themselves, the British ultimately gave up and sailed away. Colonel William Moultrie commanded the Patriot force that day, and the fort was later named Fort Moultrie in honor of his rousing victory.

Q. What colonial act of patriotic vandalism has come to be known by a much more genteel name?

A. The Boston Tea Party. On December 16, 1773, patriots tossed 342 containers (about 45 tons) of tea, worth roughly a million of today's dollars, into Boston Harbor to protest a British tax on tea and customs policies that unfairly favored British big business. Unfortunately, they unintentionally did this at low tide, and the crates piled up in the shallow water. The colonists had to jump overboard and actually smash the tea crates open in order to make sure the contents were ruined.

Q. What river did George Washington cross on Christmas night of 1776 to attack Hessian soldiers fighting for the British?

A. The Delaware. Washington traveled from Pennsylvania to New Jersey, just north of Trenton. The crossing took place under cover of night and during a frigid storm. Snow was falling, and ice was forming in the river, yet Washington led his troops toward a surprise attack the next morning. The Hessians were caught unawares, and after the fighting, nearly 1,000 were taken captive.

Q. During the Revolutionary War, how far west could British troops be found?

A. In 1778 George Rogers Clark, a lieutenant colonel in the Virginia militia, captured British troops in Illinois territory. Famous frontier explorer Daniel Boone did the same in Kentucky territory.

Q. The official state hero of Connecticut said, "I only regret that I have but one life to lose for my country." Who is he?

A. Nathan Hale. A teacher who became a spy for General George Washington during the Revolutionary War, Hale was captured by British soldiers and hanged in 1776. His famous last words inspired the new nation.

Q. What was the name of George Washington's family home?

A. Mount Vernon. Considered by many as the most famous private home in the country, this estate in Virginia created an architectural legacy. Its two-story portico, which Washington designed himself, is the most widely copied architectural technique in American history. Throughout the nation, banks, schools, government buildings, and private homes alike have mimicked this architectural style of Washington's home.

★ The town of Accident, Maryland, traces its history to 1750 when a local named George Deakins accepted 600 acres from King George II of England in relief of a debt. Deakins sent out two independent surveying parties—neither of which was aware of the other—to find the best 600 acres in the county. By coincidence, they both surveyed the same plot, beginning at the same tree. Confident that no one else owned the property, Deakins named the tract the "Accident Tract."

Q. In late 1777 George Washington needed somewhere to encamp his troops for the winter. Why did he choose to settle in at Valley Forge?

A. The location was easy to defend while protecting the convening Congress. Despite Washington's reasons for choosing this site near Philadelphia, the barren lands provided little shelter from the winter, and many soldiers froze

to death or starved from lack of food. By February 1778, however, the army began to regroup.

"British oppression has effaced the boundaries of the several colonies; the distinctions between Virginians, Pennsylvanians, New Yorkers, and New Englanders are no more. I am not a Virginian, but an American."
—Patrick Henry

Q. Where did General George Cornwallis surrender to George Washington, effectively ending the American Revolution?

A. Yorktown, Virginia. Cornwallis had retreated to coastal Virginia from North Carolina and waited to be resupplied. While the French navy closed off the sea route to British reinforcements, Washington arrived with his army from New York to trap Cornwallis against the seashore. After a siege lasting about three weeks (and which featured frequent artillery duels and trench raids), Cornwallis surrendered. At the ceremony of surrender at

Yorktown, Cornwallis's subordinate tried to hand his sword to French General Comte Jean de Rochambeau. The French officer deferred the honor to his superior officer, General Washington.

Q. Following the triumph of the Revolution, there remained the issue of what the country's new government would govern and how it would do so. A new constitution needed to be considered. Where was the Continental Convention of 1787 held?

A. Philadelphia. Among the 55 delegates present were not-yet-president George Washington, Ben Franklin, Alexander Hamilton, and James Madison. Tossing the ineffective Articles of Confederation from 1781 into the wastebasket, they built a new and stronger form of government. The eventual result was the Constitution (and the accompanying Bill of Rights) and the basis of governmental structure and operation that still runs today.

Q. The capital of the United States moved to Washington, D.C., in 1800. Where was it immediately before that?

A. Philadelphia. A rivalry between Northern and Southern advocates who each pushed to have the capital in one of their regional states had delayed the decision of a permanent location. In 1790 a compromise finally resolved the dispute, deciding that the capital would not be a part of any state. A site on the Potomac River was chosen and declared to be the District of Columbia. New York had been the nation's first capital, but as part of the compromise, the title moved to Philadelphia until the new capital was ready. Construction of the White House began in Washington in 1792, with work on the Capitol starting the following year.

Dates of Statehood for the Original 13

* * * * * * * * * * * *

1. Delaware: December 7, 1787
2. Pennsylvania: December 12, 1787
3. New Jersey: December 18, 1787
4. Georgia: January 2, 1788
5. Connecticut: January 9, 1788
6. Massachusetts: February 6, 1788
7. Maryland: April 28, 1788
8. South Carolina: May 23, 1788
9. New Hampshire: June 21, 1788
10. Virginia: June 25, 1788
11. New York: July 26, 1788
12. North Carolina: November 21, 1789
13. Rhode Island: May 29, 1790

Q. How old is the White House?

A. The White House is more than 200 years old. Built between 1792 and 1800, it followed the architectural plans of James Hoban, but it has been expanded over the years. The president and the first family live in the main part of the building, while the president's offices are in the West Wing, which is connected to the Executive Residence by a colonnade originally designed by Thomas Jefferson.

Q. Where was the Whiskey Rebellion?

A. Southwestern Pennsylvania. In 1791 Congress passed the Whiskey Act, taxing domestically distilled liquors. Citizens didn't like this tax any more than the British taxes they'd rebelled against 15 years earlier and refused to pay. In July 1794 Secretary of the Treasury Alexander Hamilton sent a U.S. marshal to southwestern Pennsylvania to serve writs upon tax scofflaws. The populace revolted and took up arms. After a few exchanges of gunfire and two rebel fatalities, the small federal garrison in the area surrendered. The rebels then burned two tax collectors' homes, robbed a mail wagon, beat up other tax collectors, and braced for a greater confrontation. President George Washington sent nearly 13,000 federalized militia soldiers west, but they received no trial of arms when the rebellion dissipated and the ringleaders fled.

Q. The British burned down the Library of Congress in 1814. Fortunately, a new replacement collection was quickly made available. Where did it come from?

A. Monticello. Thomas Jefferson sold his personal book collection, consisting of approximately 6,500 volumes, to the U.S. Congress.

Q. Where was Francis Scott Key when he began writing "The Star-Spangled Banner"?

A. On a British naval ship in Chesapeake Bay. On September 13, 1814, the British were attacking Baltimore to gain control of its port. Key and an American military officer were aboard a truce ship negotiating the release of a doctor captured by the British. Although that mission was a success, Key and his two companions were held on that ship until the barrage against Baltimore reached an end. At first light the next morning, Key saw that the American flag continued to fly above Fort McHenry, meaning that the British attack had failed. He began writing his poem to commemorate that fact before he left the British ship.

THE STATES

★ ★ ★ ★ ★ ★ ★ ★ ★ ★ ★ ★

America is made up of 50 states, and each one of them is unique. Each state has its own rich history, its own character, its own quirks, and, of course, its own trivia. How much do you know about the individual states?

Q. Which state is the birthplace of the highest number of U.S. presidents?

A. Virginia has been the motherland of eight future executives-in-chief: George Washington, Thomas Jefferson, James Madison, James Monroe, William Henry Harrison, John Tyler, Zachary Taylor, and Woodrow Wilson.

★ Ohio is the only state to be the birthplace of three successive presidents (Ulysses S. Grant, Rutherford B. Hayes, and James Garfield).

Q. Only one U.S. state has had the flags of six nations flying over it. Which state is it?

A. Texas. The nations that have controlled it over the years are Spain, France, Mexico, the Republic of Texas, the United States, and the Confederate States of America.

Q. What was the nation's first state park?

A. Niagara Falls in New York, which was given that honor in 1885. The first known European to see the falls was the Franciscan friar Louis Hennepin, in 1677. Today a total of 3,160 tons of water flow over the falls every second. Approximately 140 of the park's 400-plus acres are underwater.

In 1729 the government of Maine passed a law forbidding the use of tomatoes in any clam chowder made in the state. Since then, all New England clam chowders have been made with cream.

Q. How did California get its name?

A. Scholars believe it came from an early 16th-century work of fiction. *Las Sergas de Esplandián* by Garci Rodríguez de Montalvo tells the story of a force of Amazons led by Queen Calafia of the island of California, which

> ★★★ **FAST FACT** ★★★
> California boasts the oldest known living tree—a Bristlecone Pine named Methuselah, which is estimated to be about 4,850 years old.

was described as being near the Terrestrial Paradise, an island overflowing with gold. Many early Spanish explorers came to the New World in search of such a paradise, and for a short time they thought they might have found it in California.

Q. What state holds the nation's gold reserve?

A. Kentucky. In 1936 construction began on the U.S. Bullion Reserve, using land adjacent to the Fort Knox army base in Fort Knox, Kentucky. Workers used over 1,400 tons of steel and 16,000 cubic feet of granite. The massive, more than 20-ton bombproof door to its vault is locked with a multifactor authen-

A State by Any Other Name

* * * * * * * * * * * *

Here are few names that states were known by before they joined the union.

1. Delaware—Lower Counties on Delaware
2. Connecticut—Connecticut Colony
3. Rhode Island—Colony of Rhode Island and Providence Plantations
4. Vermont—Province of New York and New Hampshire Grants
5. Kentucky—Virginia (Kentucky County)
6. Tennessee—Province of North Carolina, Southwest Territory
7. Ohio—Northwest Territory
8. Maine—Massachusetts
9. Texas—Republic of Texas
10. California—California Republic
11. Oregon—Oregon Territory
12. Hawaii—Kingdom of Hawaii, Republic of Hawaii

tication lock that requires ten different Fort Knox employees to input a fraction of a larger combination; each employee's fraction is known only to that employee.

Q. Where can you most commonly find Cajuns?

A. In the bayous of Louisiana. In the mid-18th century, British forces moved the French-speaking settlers away from the Acadia region of the northeastern United States and Canada. These Acadians drifted down to New Orleans and the surrounding Louisiana territory, which was still under the rule of France. There they settled in the towns and wetlands of southern

State Nicknames—New England

★ ★ ★ ★ ★ ★ ★ ★ ★ ★ ★ ★

It may be part of the American character to give something a nickname. All the states have them. Some of these nicknames are official, having been voted on by the state legislature. In other cases, when nicknames haven't been a priority for state governments, the nicknames are simply informal.

- The official nickname of Connecticut is "The Constitution State," although it is commonly known as "The Nutmeg State," as well.

- Maine's state nickname? "The Pine Tree State."

- "The Bay State" is another name for Massachusetts.

- New Hampshire once had a strong quarrying industry, which provided its nickname, "The Granite State."

- Rhode Island is "The Ocean State." Although it's the smallest state in the union, it is home to more than 400 miles of coastline. With Narragansett Bay cutting about halfway into its territory, you can never be more than 30 minutes away from salt water in Rhode Island.

- Vermont is known as "The Green Mountain State," which only makes sense. *Vert mont* is French for "green mountain."

Louisiana, intermixing with American Indians and colonists of other European descent, largely isolated from the rest of the world. These "Cajuns" developed their own language and culture independent from the rest of the country.

Q. What state capital is also known as "Music City, USA"?

A. Nashville, Tennessee. Home of the Grand Ole Opry, Nashville is the traditional base for the country music industry. In the late 1800s and early 1900s, a new style of music featuring banjos, fiddles, and guitars began to gain popularity in the American South. It had developed among the hill people of Appalachia and other rural areas. Though this genre was originally known derogatorily as *hillbilly music*, it soon evolved into its own distinct genre, termed *country*.

Q. Nashville, Tennessee, was once known by a different name. What was it?

A. Before the Revolutionary War, the site was known as Big Salt Lick.

State Nicknames—Mid-Atlantic
★ ★ ★ ★ ★ ★ ★ ★ ★ ★ ★ ★

- Delaware calls itself "The First State," commemorating the fact that, on December 7, 1787, its legislature ratified the U.S. Constitution before any other state.

- Maryland's nickname goes back to the Revolutionary War. "The Old Line State" refers to Maryland's regiments fighting in the Battle of Long Island.

- New Jersey is "The Garden State," though no one can quite explain how it got that name.

- In 1785 George Washington referred to New York as "the Seat of Empire." From there, it's an easy jump to "The Empire State."

- For reasons not entirely clear, Pennsylvania is called "The Keystone State." This name likely goes back to the 1700s.

State Nicknames—Midwest

★ ★ ★ ★ ★ ★ ★ ★ ★ ★ ★ ★

- The nickname of Illinois is "The Prairie State," although "Land of Lincoln" has been a popular name on state license plates.

- Indiana is known as "The Hoosier State." But what's a Hoosier?

- Iowa's nickname is "The Hawkeye State."

- Kansas is "The Sunflower State." It may come as no surprise, then, that the Kansas state flower is the sunflower.

- Michigan is called "The Wolverine State," although "The Great Lakes State" is also popular.

- Minnesota is "The North Star State," after the state motto, *L'etoile du Nord,* which means "Star of the North."

- The most popular nickname for Missouri is "The Show Me State," although that is not an official nickname. According to Missouri's Office of the Secretary of State, it indicates "the stalwart, conservative, noncredulous character of Missourians."

- What will you find in Nebraska? Corn. Filled with people who can husk all that corn, Nebraska is called "The Cornhusker State."

- One nickname for North Dakota is "The Peace Garden State," referring to the International Peace Garden shared by North Dakota and the Canadian province of Manitoba.

- Ohio is famously "The Buckeye State"—it has an awful lot of buckeye trees, which are the official state tree.

- The nickname of South Dakota is "The Mount Rushmore State," for obvious reasons. That nickname replaced "The Sunshine State," a name that had originally been featured on the state flag.

- Wisconsin's nickname, "The Badger State," remains unofficial, but the badger is the state's official animal, and it also serves as the mascot of the University of Wisconsin.

Q. Although the Amish can be found in various areas around the United States, there is one particular county in one particular state that is especially known as their home. Can you name it?

A. Lancaster County, Pennsylvania. The Amish are a Mennonite people sometimes referred to as the Pennsylvania Dutch. Their history in the region dates back to the 18th century, after European Mennonite leader Jacob Amman split from the larger Mennonite sect within the Anabaptist movement. This new sect fled religious persecution in Europe and traveled to the United States, where they settled mostly in southeastern Pennsylvania. The Amish are prominent in the American popular mind for their refusal to use technology. Visiting an Amish community in Lancaster County is like going back in time to a pre–Industrial Revolution era. Amish farmers use hand- or horse-drawn plows, and Amish families travel in horse-drawn buggies.

> ★★★ **FAST FACT** ★★★
> St. Louis, Missouri, was the site of the first stolen car report in 1905.

TRUE OR FALSE The Minnesota Twin Cities of Minneapolis and St. Paul developed in tandem.

ANSWER False. It all began in about 1803 when the United States started building Fort Snelling in the area. Materials to build the fort and goods to live there were needed, so the port city of St. Paul blossomed about seven miles to the south. About seven miles north of the fort, there was a powerful waterfall. People made use of the power provided by that water and built lumber mills and flour mills there. The mill city of Minneapolis (then called St. Anthony) grew from that.

"The names of the States and Territories themselves form a chorus of sweet and most romantic vocables: Delaware, Ohio, Indiana, Florida, Dakota, Iowa, Wyoming, Minnesota, and the Carolinas."

—Robert Louis Stevenson

Q. What was Alaska called before it was purchased by the United States in 1867?

A. Russian America. Russia sponsored expeditions to explore its northeastern corner, and in 1741, Captain Vitus Bering sited the Alaskan mainland. Russian holdings in North America included settlements as far south as California and in the Hawaiian Islands, but Russia never put forth a concerted effort to establish actual colonies.

Q. How did the city of Nome, Alaska, get its name?

A. A British mapmaker— one with extremely poor handwriting, apparently— circled the port and wrote *Name?* next to it. Once this was misread, the new city name stuck.

★★★ **FAST FACT** ★★★

Fire ants first entered the United States in 1920 at Mobile, Alabama, on a cargo ship from South America.

Q. Which state is sometimes called the "Mother of States"?

A. Virginia. More states have been carved in total or in part from land that was once claimed by Virginia than from any other state. States that have incorporated one-time Virginia territory are Illinois, Indiana, Kentucky, Michigan, Minnesota, Ohio, West Virginia, and Wisconsin.

State Nicknames—South

★ ★ ★ ★ ★ ★ ★ ★ ★ ★ ★ ★

- Alabama has been called "The Cotton State," and "Heart of Dixie" has appeared on state license plates.

- In 1995 Arkansas officially changed its nickname from "Land of Opportunity" to "The Natural State."

- Florida's nickname is "The Sunshine State." It was first used on license plates in 1949, but the state legislature didn't make it official until 1970.

- Georgia is another state that has no nickname officially assigned by the state legislature, but it is frequently known as "The Peach State" and "The Empire State of the South."

- The nickname for Kentucky is "The Bluegrass State."

- Louisiana gets its nickname, "The Pelican State," from its state bird, the brown pelican.

- Mississippi's state flower is the magnolia, which is why many call it "The Magnolia State."

- North Carolina has been called "The Old North State," on account of it being older and further north than South Carolina, and "The Tar Heel State," although the origin of the second name is uncertain. One popular tale tells of North Carolinian soldiers in the Civil War who held their position while others retreated, due to the tar on their heels.

- South Carolina is called "The Palmetto State" after the palmetto tree, which also appears on the state flag.

- Tennessee is "The Volunteer State," a name it received when Tennesseans enthusiastically answered their governor's call for volunteers to fight the British in the War of 1812.

- As the first of the British colonies to be established in the New World, Virginia is known as "The Old Dominion."

- West Virginia calls itself "The Mountain State."

TRUE OR FALSE Rhode Island is the state with the smallest population.

ANSWER False. It's Wyoming. According to the 2010 U.S. Census, 563,626 people live in the state. There are 31 American cities with a larger population than this entire state.

Q. What was the original name of Cleveland, Ohio?

A. Cleaveland. When first incorporated as a village in 1814, the name was spelled *Cleaveland,* after founder General Moses Cleaveland. The name stuck until the early 1830s, when, as legend has it, local newspaper the *Cleveland Advertiser* dropped the *a* to fit its name on the masthead.

> ★★★ **FAST FACT** ★★★
>
> Illinois actually made it illegal to speak English for about 45 years, from the 1920s to the '60s. The law defined the official language as "American."

★ The Hammond covered bridge over Otter Creek near Pittsford, Vermont, is known as the "bridge that went on a voyage." During a flood in 1927, it came loose and floated away down the creek, ending up more than a mile downstream in the middle of a field! People moved it back in place the next winter by floating it up the creek on empty barrels and reattaching it.

Q. What can be found beneath the hilly and heavily forested landscape of Kentucky about 90 miles south-southwest of Louisville?

A. Mammoth Cave, a vast network of caves unlike anywhere else on earth. The first humans to explore the caves were Native Americans in the area some 4,000 years ago who used the caves as a burial site as well as a mine. One of the most important explorers of the caves was a slave, Stephen Bishop, who belonged to the caves' owner Franklin Gorin. During his time at Mammoth, Bishop explored more of the caves than any other modern human had, and, more importantly, he prepared maps for other explorers.

Q. What do the state of Louisiana, the Illinois Central Railroad, and Arlo Guthrie have in common?

A. The city of New Orleans. Louisiana, of course, is home to the city of New Orleans. The Illinois Central Railroad named one of its southbound trains The City of New Orleans. Musician Steve Goodman wrote a song about his travels on that train, and the song, "The City of New Orleans," became a 1972 hit for folk singer Arlo Guthrie.

State Nicknames—Southwest
★ ★ ★ ★ ★ ★ ★ ★ ★ ★ ★ ★

- Arizona's nickname is "The Grand Canyon State." We'll let you figure out why.

- Although Nevada may be most commonly known as "The Silver State," it will also answer to "The Battle-born State" and "The Sagebrush State."

- The New Mexico legislature made "Land of Enchantment" the official state nickname in 1999. It had already been appearing on license plates for 58 years by that time.

- Oklahoma is known as "The Sooner State." For a number of years, its license plates featured the slogan: "Oklahoma is OK."

- Texas is referred to as "The Lone Star State." Its state flag (which was also its national flag when Texas was a republic) has a single star in a blue field.

Q. California's Catalina Island is home to roughly 200 buffalo. How did they get there?

A. No, they didn't swim. These buffalo are descendants of a few that were taken there for a movie shoot in the 1920s and left behind.

Q. Where did the name "Texas" come from?

A. "Texas" evolved from the Caddo Indian greeting *te shas*. Since there is no *sh* sound in Spanish, early explorers and missionaries writing about their travels replaced the unfamiliar syllable with an *x* to make *te xas*.

Q. What is the nation's largest shopping facility?

A. The Mall of America, which is located in Bloomington, Minnesota, encompasses 4.2 million square feet. It employs up to 13,000 people during peak periods and houses more than 500 stores. Opened in 1992, it has developed its own tourist industry, with groups arriving from around the country and the world on a daily basis.

Q. One of the world's most famous archaeological and fossil sites is in California, right in the heart of Los Angeles. What is it?

A. The La Brea Tar Pits. As the ocean that once covered California began to recede about 100,000 years ago, older fossil fuels began to seep toward the earth's surface. In La Brea, this took the form

State Nicknames—Mountain

★ ★ ★ ★ ★ ★ ★ ★ ★ ★ ★ ★

- Colorado, which entered the union in 1876, has been called "The Centennial State."

- Although Idaho may be best known for its famous potatoes, its nickname is "The Gem State."

- Montana is called both "The Treasure State" and "The Big Sky State."

- "The Beehive State" refers to Utah. State leaders chose the beehive as the state emblem to represent industry.

- Wyoming has been known as "The Cowboy State," but more recently it has become "The Equality State" to highlight its pioneering record in women's rights.

of "asphalt," an extremely sticky, tarlike substance. It formed swamplike conditions roughly 40,000 years ago that trapped animals wandering through the area. Predators spotting them gave chase and got stuck in the asphalt themselves. The unique chemical nature of asphalt protected these animals' bones from deterioration, which gives modern-day scientists pristine examples of prehistoric mammal skeletons, such as mammoths and mastodons, American camels and American lions, and saber-toothed cats.

★ The first child born to settlers in Madison, Wisconsin—on September 14, 1837—displayed her loyalty to her territory (it wouldn't be a state for another decade) right in her name. Her mother, Roseline Peck, named her daughter Wisconsiana.

Q. Home to one of the nation's most famous Mardi Gras celebrations, it's the oldest neighborhood in the city of New Orleans, Louisiana, and one of the oldest in the entire country. What is it called?

State Nicknames—Pacific

★ ★ ★ ★ ★ ★ ★ ★ ★ ★ ★ ★

- Alaska is referred to as "The Last Frontier." Much of the land there is still a frontier.

- California is known as "The Golden State."

- Hawaii's nickname is "The Aloha State."

- "The Beaver State" is Oregon's nickname. It honors the state's official animal.

- Washington certainly has its fair share of evergreen forests, so its nickname, "The Evergreen State," comes naturally.

A. The French Quarter. It was established in 1718 by Jean Baptiste Bienville, a French Canadian military officer who devised the area as a network of 70 squares. This early French influence is still present in the street names, such as the *Rue de Bourbon*, and in the French Market near Jackson Square. In the mid-18th century, however, the Louisiana territory entered a period of Spanish rule that heavily influenced the neighborhood. Much of the quarter was rebuilt in the Spanish style during this time, featuring buildings with flat roofs, stucco walls, wrought-iron balconies, and inner courtyards.

ARTS AND LETTERS

★ ★ ★ ★ ★ ★ ★ ★ ★ ★ ★ ★ ★

The United States has a rich tradition of arts and education—books, music, architecture, colleges and universities. All have graced the nation and established its culture. Test your knowledge of such splendor with the information that follows.

Q. In 1845 Henry David Thoreau left Boston and moved to live beside what body of water?

A. Walden Pond near Concord, Massachusetts. He lived there for two years, two months, and two days, recording his experience in *Walden; or, Life in the Woods*. Later he stated famously, "I went to the woods because I wished to live deliberately, to front only the essential facts of life, and see if I could not learn what it had to teach, and not, when I came to die, discover that I had not lived."

Q. What is the Cadillac Ranch?

A. A curious car sculpture located along Interstate 40 outside Amarillo, Texas. Ten classic Caddies that span the model years 1949 to 1963 are buried halfway into the ground, nose first. It was created in 1974 by the Ant Farm, a San Francisco art collective.

★ Although Woodstock, or more correctly, An Aquarian Exposition: 3 Days of Peace & Music at the Woodstock Music & Art Fair, took its name from the town of

Woodstock, New York, it was actually held at Max Yasgur's dairy farm in Bethel, New York, 40 or 50 miles southwest of the town of Woodstock.

Q. Architect Frank Lloyd Wright's Fallingwater was built atop what natural feature?

A. A waterfall. Built in 1936 in southwestern Pennsylvania as a private residence for Pittsburgh department store magnate Edward Kaufmann, Fallingwater was immediately hailed as a tour de force. A 1991 poll by *Architectural Record* voted the house the most important building of the previous 100 years.

Q. The Institute of Musical Art, an internationally renowned school of music, dance, and drama, was founded in New York City in 1905 by Dr. Frank Damrosch. What is its name today?

A. The Juilliard School. The school was expanded after Augustus D. Juilliard, a wealthy textile merchant who died in 1919, left the single largest bequest for the advancement of American musical education of that era. In 1924 the trustees of that multimillion-dollar bequest founded the Juilliard Graduate School, which merged with Damrosch's Institute of Musical Art two years later and took the name Juilliard School of Music. Juilliard's dance division was established in 1951, and in 1968 a four-year drama division was added. The school's name was changed to the Juilliard School a year later to reflect its broadened curriculum.

⭐ The first chartered college in the American colonies—and in the New World—was Harvard. Started near Boston in 1636 as an all-male school to educate Puritan ministers, this college had only nine students and one teacher. Today it has grown in enrollment to 21,000 undergraduate and graduate-degree candidates and has become perhaps the best-known educational institution in the world. It is the alma mater of eight U.S. presidents (both Adamses, both Roosevelts, Hayes, Kennedy, Obama, and George W. Bush).

Q. How can you stick one toe in the Hudson River and another in the Atlantic Ocean at the same time or go from the Bronx to Coney Island in just one step?

A. By visiting the New York City Panorama, the world's largest architectural model of a city. Built for the 1964 World's Fair, the model measures 9,335 square feet and contains some 895,000 tiny buildings, streets, parks, bridges, homes, and waterways. One inch equals 100 feet, so the Empire State Building is almost 15 inches tall. At the time of the panorama's creation, it carried a $672,000 price tag. But in 1992, when it was updated to reflect the changing skyline, the remodel cost around $750,000.

★★★ **FAST FACT** ★★★

In 1980, the state of Ohio contained more universities than the entire African continent.

Q. Where was the intended audience for the earliest book-of-the-month club inclined to live?

A. New York bookseller Harry Scherman started such a club in 1926 to target people who lived in remote areas or were just too busy to keep up with new releases. The first selection was *Lolly Willows, or The Loving Huntsman* by Sylvia Townsend Warner, which was sent to 5,000 readers.

Q. What painting did officials in Holmes County, Ohio, once put into incarceration?

A. *Behalt* by Heinz Gaugel. In 1978 Gaugel began work on a 10- by 265-foot cyclorama depicting Anabaptist life and history. A year later, however, the main financial backer died, and her heirs bickered with Gaugel over ownership. When the dispute headed to court, the sheriff stored the painting safely in a jail cell. Gaugel ultimately won the fight and finished his massive painting in 1992.

Q. Where and what was Tin Pan Alley?

A. From the late 19th century to the early 20th, the West 28th Street district in lower Manhattan between Fifth and Sixth Avenues came to be known as Tin Pan Alley and produced hit songs including "In the Good Old Summertime," "Alexander's Ragtime Band," "By the Light of the Silvery Moon," "Take Me Out to the Ball Game," and "Happy Days Are Here Again." Newspaperman Monroe Rosenfeld coined the term after hearing the dissonant sound of multiple composers simultaneously pounding on pianos in the area, or so the story goes. Those composers included legends such as Irving Berlin, Hoagy Carmichael, Scott Joplin, Cole Porter, and George and Ira Gershwin, and now their music itself carries the name Tin Pan Alley.

Q. Where did Mark Twain land his first job as a writer?

A. In 1862 Samuel Clemens took a job as a reporter for the *Virginia City Territorial Enterprise* in Nevada. It was his first job as a writer and his first occasion to use the pen name Mark Twain. He later included vivid (if exaggerated) descriptions of Virginia City in his book *Roughing It.*

Q. During the Roaring Twenties, brash young voices of exuberance were heard, sometimes being called the black Literary Renaissance or the New Negro Movement. What was the more common name of this phenomenon?

A. The Harlem Renaissance. An unexpected confluence of writers, dramatists, musicians, artists, and sociologists in the New York neighborhood of Harlem—as well as their wealthy white patrons—instigated an intellectual revolution. Principal artists included Langston Hughes (whose defining essay "The Negro Artist and the Racial Mountain" is sometimes credited with sparking the movement), Zora Neale Hurston, Claude McKay, Jean Toomer, and Alaine Locke, the first African American Rhodes scholar. Others insist that the Harlem Renaissance cannot be understood without Duke Ellington and Marcus Mosiah Garvey.

> ★ ★ ★ **FAST FACT** ★ ★ ★
>
> The *Merriam-Webster Dictionary* was once banned in Carlsbad, New Mexico, because it was believed to contain obscene words.

Q. What museum has the largest Impressionist and Post-Impressionist collections in the United States?

A. The Art Institute of Chicago. Founded in 1879, the Art Institute has actually gathered the largest collection of Impressionist and Post-Impressionist work outside the Musée d'Orsay in Paris. The massive collection includes works by Renoir, Monet, Degas, Seurat, and Gauguin, among others.

Q. Where was the first American kindergarten?

A. Watertown, Wisconsin. In 1856 Mrs. Margarethe Schurz, a German immigrant from Hamburg, founded the first U.S. kindergarten in her home. The racket drove her husband nuts, so she soon moved the kindergarten to a nearby frame building.

Q. What Oklahoma City museum bills itself as "America's premier institution of Western history, art and culture"?

A. The National Cowboy & Western Heritage Museum. Originally established in 1955 as the National Cowboy Hall of Fame and Museum, this institution has seen more than 10 million visitors pass through its doors over the years.

Q. The Beats were a group of countercultural writers and poets that coalesced during the 1940s and '50s. What places were known as popular Beat hangouts?

A. New York City's Greenwich Village, North Beach in San Francisco, and Venice in Los Angeles. Rebelling against the postwar ranch-house-with-basement model of social conformity, they glorified rootlessness, creativity, and travel for travel's sake. Prominent members of the Beat movement included Jack Kerouac, Allen Ginsberg, and William S. Burroughs.

Q. Where can you find a full-size replica of the Parthenon?

A. Nashville, Tennessee. Built for the Tennessee Centennial Exposition in 1897 as a reflection of the city's nickname, "The Athens of the South," it was never intended to be permanent, but it became so popular at the exposition that it was not torn down. A few years later the building's temporary nature became undeniable, so it was rebuilt in concrete to become a permanent Nashville fixture.

★ New York City's Chelsea neighborhood is home to more than 370 art galleries. Outside Manhattan, the greatest concentration of art galleries in the United States is in Chicago's River North area.

Q. What was the Brill Building?

A. It was an office building at 1619 Broadway in New York City where many of the most popular songs of the 1950s and '60s were created. Although mostly known for its writers, the building contained music publishing companies, recording studios, and promoters. Songs written here include "Jailhouse Rock" (Jerry Leiber and Mike Stoller), "Save the Last Dance for Me" (Doc Pomus and Mort Shuman), "One Fine Day" (Gerry Goffin and Carole King), "We Gotta Get Out of This Place" (Barry Mann and Cynthia Weil), and "Do Wah Diddy Diddy" (Ellie Greenwich and Jeff Barry).

"Every day we squeezed into our respective cubby holes with just enough room for a piano, a bench, and maybe a chair for the lyricist if you were lucky. You'd sit there and write and you could hear someone in the next cubby hole composing a song exactly like yours."
—Carole King on life at the Brill Building

Q. Brilliantly lit with clusters of magnificent theaters, this street is known the world over as "The Great White Way." What is it?

The Top Ten U.S. Universities (by enrollment)

★ ★ ★ ★ ★ ★ ★ ★ ★ ★ ★

1. Arizona State University, Tempe, Arizona (est. 1885)
2. University of Central Florida, Orlando, Florida (est. 1963)
3. The Ohio State University, Columbus, Ohio (est. 1870)
4. University of Texas at Austin, Austin, Texas (est. 1883)
5. University of Florida, Gainesville, Florida (est. 1853)
6. University of Minnesota, Minneapolis/St. Paul, Minnesota (est. 1851)
7. Michigan State University, East Lansing, Michigan (est. 1855)
8. Texas A&M University, College Station, Texas (est. 1871)
9. Pennsylvania State University, University Park, Pennsylvania (est. 1855)
10. University of Michigan, Ann Arbor, Michigan (est. 1817)

A. Broadway. In the mid-19th century, the thoroughfare transformed New York City into the foremost center for live stage entertainment in America. From about 20 Broadway theaters in 1900, the number of venues grew to an all-time high of 80 by 1925. During the record-setting 1927–28 Broadway season, theatergoers had their choice of more than 250 shows.

Q. What do Aaron Copland's *Billy the Kid*, Willa Cather's *Death Comes for the Archbishop*, Thornton Wilder's *Our Town*, Alice Sebold's *The Lovely Bones*, and Michael Chabon's *The Adventures of Kavalier and Clay* all have in common?

A. Their creators worked on each of them at the MacDowell Colony. Founded in 1907 by Marian and Edward MacDowell, the colony is a nonprofit institution located in

Peterborough, New Hampshire, that operates as a retreat for writers, visual artists, composers, photographers, filmmakers, sculptors, and architects.

Q. What was the nation's first coeducational college?

A. Oberlin College in Oberlin, Ohio. Founded in 1833 by Presbyterian minister John J. Shipherd and missionary Philo P. Stewart, Oberlin accepted its first female students into the previously all-male baccalaureate program in 1837. Oberlin was also progressive in matters of race, admitting black students as early as 1835.

TRUE OR FALSE The movie, TV show, and off-Broadway play *Fame* were inspired by an actual high school.

ANSWER True. New York City's LaGuardia High School of Music & Art and Performing Arts has produced more notable performers than any other high school in the land, including Al Pacino, Jennifer Aniston, Wesley Snipes, Adrien Brody, Béla Fleck, Eartha Kitt, and Isaac Mizrahi. LaGuardia is much like any other high school, with a rigorous curriculum of college prep courses in math, science, and English, but students also practice their particular discipline—whether it be acting, dance, or music—for three to four hours each day.

★ Among all the works of modern art on view at New York City's Guggenheim Museum, the great masterpiece is the building itself. Frank Lloyd Wright designed a round building that bobs like a cork in a sea of square structures along Fifth Avenue. Visitors inside the building start at the top and stroll downward along a continuous spiral ramp whose walls are lined with paintings.

THE MILITARY

* * * * * * * * * * * *

America is blessed with a proud military tradition. It has also been blessed to have been free from attack by foreign powers throughout most of its history. But there has been some military activity within these borders. What do you know about it?

Q. When was the Pentagon built?

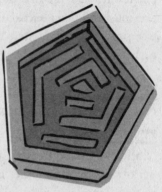

A. Ground was broken on September 11, 1941, and construction was completed just 16 months later, on January 15, 1943. Some 4,000 workers toiled in three shifts during the beginning years of World War II to complete the building at a cost of $83 million. It is a huge structure, with more than 17.5 miles of corridors, yet its design allows a person to reach any point in the building from any other within seven minutes.

Q. Which war saw the Battle of Lake Erie?

A. The War of 1812. On September 10, 1813, an American flotilla under Commodore Oliver H. Perry faced a British flotilla off modern-day Sandusky, Ohio, for control of the Great Lakes. The Americans' shorter-range but heavier cannon dictated the need to fight the British at close quarters. Perry's flagship, USS *Lawrence*, was beaten to a pulp by HMS *Detroit*, but Perry transferred his flag to USS *Niagara* and continued the battle there. Perry cut loose with both broadsides, and the two British ships, *Queen Charlotte* and *Detroit,* collided in the confusion. After three hours of battle, the British were captured.

Q. President Franklin Roosevelt called December 7, 1941, "a date which will live in infamy." What happened on that day?

A. The Japanese attacked the U.S. naval base at Pearl Harbor. Hawaii was still a territory at the time, but Americans reacted as if it had been an assault on the mainland. The attack—launched without benefit of a formal declaration of war—sank or heavily damaged 18 warships, destroyed nearly 200 aircraft, and killed 2,400 U.S. servicepeople.

> ★★★ **FAST FACT** ★★★
>
> Japanese pilots who attacked Pearl Harbor had studied postcards provided by spy Takeoyoshi Yoshikawa that showed where U.S. ships were normally positioned in the harbor.

TRUE OR FALSE No civilians were killed during the Japanese attack on Pearl Harbor.

ANSWER False. While the largest loss of life at Pearl Harbor occurred when the forward magazine on the battleship USS *Arizona* exploded, a little-known or largely forgotten fact about the attack is that at least 48 civilians were also killed by exploding shells and flying shrapnel.

★ On June 8, 1959, the USS *Barbero* submarine fired a 36-foot Regulus 1 winged missile at Mayport Auxiliary Station in Florida—to deliver the mail. This was the first recorded use of missile mail, which carried 3,000 letters addressed to President Dwight D. Eisenhower and other government officials.

Q. Where did the Quartering Act of 1765 allow British troops to sleep?

A. In colonists' homes. This was one of what colonists considered "The Intolerable Acts" that brought about the American Revolution. In New York City in 1766, 1,500 British troops were refused quarters and forced to remain on their ships. As a matter of fact, the Founders felt so strongly about the act of quartering that they limited it in the Bill of Rights. In its entirety, the Third Amendment to the U.S. Constitution reads: "No Soldier shall, in time of peace be quartered in any house, without the consent of the Owner, nor in time of war, but in a manner to be prescribed by law."

Q. Are there aliens living in Area 51?

A. Not officially. Because of the secretive nature of this restricted testing site and airfield controlled by the U.S. military near Rachel, Nevada, little has been confirmed about the actual goings-on at the base, and conspiracy theories abound. In 1947, an unidentified flying object crashed in Roswell, New Mexico, and some conspiracy theorists believe that Area 51 houses the alien spaceship recovered there in secret hangars. Other conjecture includes the idea that it houses alien life-forms, as well. The government does little to dispel such theories. What *is* known, however, is that the base was a testing site for the Lockheed-Martin Corporation's

U-2 spy plane in the early 1950s and that it has been the testing site for dozens of other projects, including the Stealth Bomber.

Q. Where was the headquarters for the Manhattan Project?

A. Although World War II's Manhattan Project in the early 1940s is often associated with Los Alamos, New Mexico, it actually had major facilities there and at two other sites: Oak Ridge, Tennessee, and Hanford, Washington.

★★★ **FAST FACT** ★★★

During Oak Ridge's annual Secret City Festival (so named because the research was top secret) visitors can tour Manhattan Project sites to see where the bomb was devised.

Each site was to have a different function: Oak Ridge was to refine uranium-235 using an enormous electromagnet; Hanford, chosen for its proximity to the Columbia River's limitless supply of cooling water, raced to build a reactor capable of making plutonium-239; and Los Alamos figured out how to build the fissile material into bombs.

The September 11, 2001, attacks against the World Trade Center and the Pentagon all happened within one hour. The first plane hit the World Trade Center's North Tower at 8:46 A.M. Seventeen minutes later, at 9:03 A.M., the second plane hit the South Tower. Just over half an hour after that, at 9:37 A.M., the third plane hit the Pentagon. The final plane, which crashed in a field near Shanksville, Pennsylvania, went down at 10:03 A.M.

TRUE OR FALSE The area in and around Columbia University in New York City was once the site of a Revolutionary War battle.

ANSWER True. A modest plaque on Columbia's Mathematics Building notes that on September 16, 1776, the area was the site of the bloody Battle of Harlem Heights, a fierce skirmish between George Washington's Continental Army and seasoned British troops. After an unplanned and unanticipated fight, an American victory there encouraged the ragtag Continental soldiers to believe that they could actually win a war against the greatest military power on earth.

Q. Where is the Knox Trail?

A. In upstate New York and Massachusetts. In late 1775 General George Washington called on General Henry Knox to retrieve cannons from abandoned forts in upstate New York. Over six weeks, Knox and his troops hauled 60 tons of cannons and other armaments on oxen- and horse-drawn sleds across some 300 miles of frozen rivers and the snow-covered Berkshire Mountains to Boston. The city was on the verge of being besieged by the British, but when the Redcoats saw how heavily

The Five U.S. Armed Forces Service Academies

★ ★ ★ ★ ★ ★ ★ ★ ★ ★ ★ ★ ★

1. The U.S. Military Academy, West Point, New York, founded on March 16, 1802.

2. The U.S. Naval Academy, Annapolis, Maryland, founded on October 10, 1845.

3. The U.S. Coast Guard Academy, New London, Connecticut, established on July 31, 1876.

4. The U.S. Merchant Marine Academy, Kings Point, New York, dedicated on September 30, 1943.

5. The U.S. Air Force Academy, Colorado Springs, Colorado, founded on April 1, 1954.

Forts of New York

* * * * * * * * * * * *

Rarely do people associate military bases with New York City, but it is home to more than 20 historic forts and Army bases. Here are five—one in each borough.

1. **Blockhouse #1 (Manhattan):** At the northern end of Central Park, the remains of Blockhouse #1 tower over the landscape, flag flying high. Built by volunteers in 1814 to protect New York from the British, the stone building never saw action.

2. **Fort Hamilton (Brooklyn):** An active Army base and site of the Harbor Defense Museum, Fort Hamilton played key roles in the Revolutionary War and the War of 1812. The current fort was constructed in 1825, and Robert E. Lee was stationed there in 1841. Two decades later, it served as a training site for volunteers fighting Lee's forces during the Civil War.

3. **Fort Schuyler (Bronx):** Currently home to SUNY Maritime College and the Maritime Industry Museum, the site was bombarded by the British during the Revolutionary War. Construction on the current gray stone fort began in 1833. It was used as a prison during the Civil War and as a training ground for World War I doughboys.

4. **Fort Tilden (Queens):** Now an arts center, nature reserve, and the anchor of the most unpopulated stretch of beach in New York City, Fort Tilden was established in 1917 to defend against attack by air or sea. It was decommissioned in 1974.

5. **Fort Wadsworth (Staten Island):** The real estate occupied by Fort Wadsworth has seen the longest continuous military use in the United States. Fortified by the Dutch in the 1600s, the site was occupied by the British during the Revolution and then run by various branches of the U.S. military until it closed in 1994.

fortified Boston Harbor was with the newly installed weapons, they withdrew their troops. Today, the Knox Trail, which is dotted with a series of plaques along Knox's original route, commemorates these heroic efforts.

TRUE OR FALSE The Japanese military launched a second attack on Pearl Harbor only a few months after the first one that had been so successful for them.

ANSWER True. In Operation K, two planes—each carrying four 550-pound bombs—flew from the Marshall Islands toward their intended target of the Pearl Harbor naval docks. Unbeknownst to the pilots, however, U.S. radar stations in Hawaii had already spotted them as potential bogies while they were still some distance away. Air-raid alarms were sounded on Pearl Harbor, and fighters scrambled to intercept the planes. One Japanese plane dropped

★★★ **FAST FACT** ★★★

Boise City, Oklahoma, was inadvertently bombed on July 5, 1943, when a B-17 pilot mistook the lights on the town square for his training target.

its bombs on the slopes of Oahu's Mount Tantalus; the other dropped its payload into the ocean at the entrance to Pearl Harbor. Ultimately, however, U.S. fighter pilots, radar operators, and ground controllers lost the Japanese aircraft as they banked back toward the west.

★ During the Vietnam era, the 111th Tactical Recon Squadron, Texas Air National Guard became known as "Air Canada" for the number of Vietnam-dodging VIPs who served there. At that time, the National Guard was used primarily for domestic duty and was rarely—if ever—deployed overseas, so service there was widely seen as a way to fulfill military service without encountering an actual shooting war. This was how some politicians' sons and Dallas Cowboys avoided walking point in the A Shau Valley.

"Here rests in honored glory an American soldier known but to God."

—Inscription upon the Tomb of the Unknowns
at Arlington National Cemetery

TRUE OR FALSE No bombs were dropped on the U.S. mainland during World War II.

ANSWER False. In 1944 and 1945 the Japanese sent thousands of balloon bombs aloft to float to the United States where they might start fires or otherwise create havoc. Although these balloons were largely ineffective, a balloon bomb in Oregon claimed the lives of a minister's wife and five children from the Sunday school. Another exploded near the Boeing plant in Seattle that produced B-29s, and a third shorted a high-tension wire, temporarily blacking out one of the Manhattan Project's reactors in Hanford, Washington.

Q. Nearly a decade before the Japanese bombed Pearl Harbor, another nation launched an attack against the site. What country was it?

A. The United States. Instead of an actual attack, however, U.S. Navy Rear Admiral Harry Yarnell launched a surprise mock attack on February 7, 1932, that hypothetically knocked stationary U.S. aircraft out of commission and sunk or damaged a multitude of warships. After the exercise, some admirals argued for a reassessment of naval tactics, but the notion was voted down. Japanese observers who had witnessed the American exercise forwarded a report to Tokyo. It concluded: "In case the enemy's main fleet is berthed at Pearl Harbor, the idea should be to open hostilities by surprise attack from the air."

NATIONAL EXPANSION

★ ★ ★ ★ ★ ★ ★ ★ ★ ★ ★

The frontier—whether defined by the Appalachian Mountains and the Mississippi River or the Pacific Ocean and Arctic ice—has always held a special place in the American imagination. Test your knowledge about the edges of the United States as they were pushed further and further.

Q. The most significant cattle drives in the Old West took place along the rugged and historic Chisholm Trail. What two cities did the Chisholm Trail connect?

A. San Antonio, Texas, and Abilene, Kansas. Jesse Chisholm, who was half-Scot and half-Cherokee, mapped out a route in 1867 for cattle breeders to move livestock north for shipping east. Winding through Indian Territory and crossing the dangerous Red River, the trip took about four months. By the mid-1880s, railroads had been put through, and the Chisholm Trail was no longer necessary.

Q. Meriwether Lewis and William Clark were renowned American explorers. What did they explore?

A. The Louisiana Territory. When President Thomas Jefferson added 828,000 square miles to the nation in 1803, he wanted to

know what he'd bought. Lewis and Clark and their "Corps of Discovery"—23 soldiers, three interpreters, and one slave—set out from St. Louis, Missouri, on May 19, 1804. They took one

15 Animals First Identified by Lewis and Clark

★ ★ ★ ★ ★ ★ ★ ★ ★ ★ ★ ★

Lewis and Clark's Corps of Discovery did much more than simply map new territory. They also had a scientific mission: to find and identify new North American plants and animals. By the end of their trek, they had found and identified more than 100 new animals and over 175 new types of plants. Here are 15 of their most prominent animal discoveries.

1. American Raven
2. Channel Catfish
3. Coyote
4. Ermine
5. Grizzly Bear
6. Harbor Seal
7. Mountain Goat
8. Mountain Lion
9. Pacific Loon
10. Prairie Rattlesnake
11. Red Fox
12. Sea Otter
13. Steelhead Trout
14. Western Common Crow
15. White-Tailed Deer

large keelboat and two canoes. On November 7, 1805, they first saw the Pacific Ocean in present-day Oregon. They returned to St. Louis on September 23, 1806, having traveled more than 8,000 miles. Among their numerous discoveries was the fact that North America was more than 1,200 miles wider than previously believed.

Q. How much did the United States pay to Napoleon's France for the Louisiana Purchase?

A. $15 million (in today's purchasing power, about $294 million). Thomas Jefferson's administration closed the deal on December 20, 1803, affectively doubling the nation's territory.

Q. Where was the golden spike driven to connect the first transcontinental railroad in 1869?

A. Promontory Summit, Utah. The Union Pacific and the Central Pacific railroads each built track from one side of the country toward the middle, finally meeting on May 10, 1869.

TRUE OR FALSE The ten-gallon hat was invented in Texas.

ANSWER False. John Stetson was a well-known Philadelphia haberdasher who needed something to boost business. He knew that cattle barons from the big state of Texas liked everything king-size, so he designed the broad-brimmed, tall-crowned ten-gallon Western cowboy hat (which can really only hold about one gallon). The hat became known as "The Boss of the Plains" and was the standard for cowboys for years.

Dr. Edwin James was the first to climb Colorado's famous Pikes Peak, reaching the summit in 1820. His feat was recognized by having the mountain named James Peak in his honor. Unfortunately

★★★ FAST FACT ★★★

Old West outlaw Billy the Kid was born in New York City.

for James, however, he didn't capture the public imagination as much as the initial non-Native American explorer to have spotted the mountain in the first place 14 years earlier: Zebulon Montgomery Pike. Even though Pike had tried to climb to the summit himself but had failed, his was the name people remembered. By the 1850s the site was so commonly referred to as Pikes Peak that the name was officially changed.

Q. What was "Seward's Folly"?

A. In 1867 Secretary of State William Seward bought the Alaska territory from Russia. He was ridiculed for wasting the nation's money on what was considered little more than "a large lump of ice." The price Seward paid—$7,200,000—worked out to about two cents an acre.

Q. How long was the Pony Express in existence?

A. Only 19 months. In 1860 the Pony Express mail service cut the amount of time for mail delivery from St. Joseph, Missouri, to Sacramento, California, from about three weeks to just eight days. Riders took mail by horseback, and changing stations were spaced at specific intervals where riders and their cargo could be switched. In October 1861, however, telegraph lines reached San Francisco, and the Pony Express was obsolete.

★ Daniel Boone helped blaze the Cumberland Gap trail from Virginia into Kentucky and Tennessee, making travel across the Appalachian Mountains accessible. Historians believe that nearly 300,000 people passed through the gap between 1760 and 1850 on their way west.

TRUE OR FALSE During the first half of the 19th century, an eccentric but kindly man roamed the western frontier of the United States planting apple seeds that became orchards that helped to feed the settlers of the region.

ANSWER True. Although he is commonly known as "Johnny Appleseed," his real name was John Chapman, and he was born in Leominster, Massachusetts, on September 26, 1774. By 1797 he had traveled to western Pennsylvania and planted his earliest recorded nursery near the Allegheny River. A kind and generous man, Chapman did have an eccentric appearance, and he really did go barefoot most of the time. He appears to have rarely settled down, instead traveling from cabin to cabin, exchanging apples, apple seeds, and medicinal plants for the food and hospitality of settlers.

Q. In 1850, San Francisco's population went from 800 people to more than 20,000. Why?

A. Gold. After gold was found on the American River on January 24, 1848, it was only a matter of time until the Gold Rush was on. The population influx was so quick that California organized itself politically and applied for statehood. It became the 31st U.S. state on September 9, 1850.

Q. Gold miners in the 1849 California Gold Rush became known as "Forty-niners," but they also had another nickname. What was it?

A. Argonauts, which means "gold travelers." The first California Argonaut might have been James Marshall, who was working as a carpenter building a sawmill for John Sutter in northern California when he discovered gold on

> ★★★ **FAST FACT** ★★★
>
> By 1855 Forty-niners in the California Gold Rush had mined $200 million worth of the precious metal.

the site. Although sworn to secrecy, Sutter's workers spread the word, and soon, gold seekers came from as far away as Australia and China. By 1852, more than 200,000 people had found their way to the Sacramento Valley, seeking the riches of gold.

Q. What is the name of the route that the Cherokee took from their native lands in Georgia and the Southeast to new lands in modern-day Oklahoma?

A. The Trail of Tears. More than 15,000 Cherokee were sent to the Indian Territory, driven by 7,000 U.S. Army troops. The forcible removal of the Cherokee from their lands began in May 1838. Despite official orders that the Cherokee were to be treated kindly, families were separated and people were given only minutes to gather their belongings. Bad weather, neglect, and limited food supplies turned the 800-mile march into a horrific trek, during which more than 4,000 Cherokee died. The survivors reached Oklahoma in March 1839.

★ A bank in Vernal, Utah, was built from bricks delivered by the U.S. Postal Service in 1916. The builders discovered that it was cheaper to mail them from Salt Lake City than it was to ship them by wagon freight.

Q. In 1870 an expedition led by Nathaniel Langford stumbled across a majestic sight: In a field of bubbling hot springs, a plume of water shot from the ground hundreds of feet into the sky. Where was this expedition?

A. It was in today's Yellowstone National Park. Langford, who would later become the park's first superintendent, had seen "Old Faithful." He was amazed not

> ★★★ **FAST FACT** ★★★
> Yellowstone became the first national park on March 1, 1872.

only by the geyser's majesty but also by its regularity—the geyser erupted at consistent intervals, shooting high into the air for several minutes at a time, earning it the nickname it has today.

Q. The Mormon religion hasn't always been based in Utah. What other sites have been important in the development of the Mormon faith?

A. Joseph Smith published *The Book of Mormon* and founded the Church of Jesus Christ of Latter-day Saints in New York in 1830. He moved the church to Ohio the next year and then trekked to Missouri. In 1839 the Mormons crossed back across the Mississippi River and established a community in Nauvoo, Illinois. After a few years, however, Smith was assassinated and the Latter Day Saints had to move on again. In 1846, under Brigham Young, the church picked up and moved west, finally settling in Utah's Salt Lake Valley.

> ★★★ **FAST FACT** ★★★
>
> The famed gunfight at the O. K. Corral was actually fought in a vacant lot off Fremont Street in Tombstone, Arizona.

Q. Now a national park in the southwest corner of Colorado, this massive honeycomb of cliff dwellings had been abandoned for some 700 years before they were rediscovered by American prospectors and miners. What is its name?

A. Mesa Verde. At one time these structures, which were built beneath the overhangs of a series of mesas, were home to the Anasazi, an ancient Pueblo people who populated the region. Around 1190 or so, the Anasazi began moving from the mesa tops to the outcroppings and cliffs below, constructing a vast network of dwellings in the alcoves beneath the cliffs. These structures were made primarily of sandstone and were often divided into many rooms that would house multiple families—the largest of these, which is known as "Cliff Palace," once housed 100 people in its 150 rooms.

Q. How did the Badlands of South Dakota get their name?

A. From the Sioux nickname for the region, *maku siku*, which means "bad land." The Sioux lived there until the late 19th century, when they were driven out by the U.S. Army to make room for homesteaders who attempted to farm the rocky, arid land. When such farming proved difficult, most of these pioneers headed further west.

Q. The Oregon Trail was a major route for pioneers heading west. Which states did it pass through?

A. The 2,000-mile route trekked through the modern-day states of Missouri, Kansas, Nebraska, Wyoming, Idaho, and Oregon to the Columbia River. Settlers could travel by boat to Independence, Missouri, which became a primary launching site for wagon trains heading west.

Q. Who mapped out the Oregon Trail?

A. John C. Fremont. He made several journeys along the trail, each time defining the way westward more clearly. The explorer eventually became one of the first two senators from California, where the city of Fremont is named for him. In 1856 Fremont was the first presidential candidate ever put forward by the Republican Party, but he lost to Democrat James Buchanan.

Q. By what other names were covered wagons known?

A. *Prairie schooners*, because their canvas coverings billowed in the wind like the sails of sea schooners.

★★★ **FAST FACT** ★★★

Covered wagons were done in by the advent of railroads in the 1870s.

These wagons formed "trains" that sometimes stretched for five miles. Covered wagons were also called *Conestogas*, after the Pennsylvania town where they were built.

Q. Why should we remember the Alamo?

A. Originally a Franciscan mission in San Antonio, the Alamo was a fort in the Texan fight against Mexico. In February 1836 General Antonio López de Santa Anna and 2,000 Mexican soldiers stormed the fort, which had only 150 defenders. The siege lasted into March, when the remaining warriors fought hand-to-hand with Mexican troops inside the garrison. All 150 Texans were killed, along with 600 Mexican soldiers. The cry "Remember the Alamo" helped defeat Santa Anna later at the Battle of San Jacinto.

Q. When scouting through today's South Dakota, Lewis and Clark reported seeing a "moving multitude which darkened the whole plains." What was it?

A. Bison or American buffalo. Estimates of the population of American buffalo when pioneers started to head west range from 30 million to 75 million. But big-game hunters, Wild West shows, and hide skinners all contributed to the demise of the animal. By the late 1880s, the population of American buffalo had dwindled to less than 1,000.

Q. One of James K. Polk's slogans in his 1844 presidential campaign was "54–40 or Fight!" What did that mean?

A. At that time, the Oregon Territory was owned and settled by both British and Americans, but Polk wanted to get rid of the British entirely. United States territory, he maintained, should extend to the latitude of 54° 40′, and he was willing to fight for it. Once he won the election, however, Polk compromised. He agreed to set the U.S. border at 49° latitude, which is where it is today. The latitude 54° 40', however, still has significance today: It is the southernmost border of Alaska.

> *"One cannot be pessimistic about the West.*
> *This is the native home of hope."*
> —Wallace Stegner, *The Sound of Mountain Water*

Q. In 1876 Lieutenant Colonel George Armstrong Custer led his 265 troops against a Lakota village at Little Bighorn. How many Native American warriors were in the village?

A. Approximately 2,500. Warriors from a number of American Indian nations came together to fight with Sitting Bull against the encroaching soldiers. Custer grossly underestimated the number of warriors encamped at the Little Bighorn River in the Montana territory and initiated the attack. Led into battle by Oglala chief Crazy Horse, among others, the warriors easily defeated Custer and wiped out his troops.

Q. Where did we get the term *red light district*?

A. It owes its origin to the colored glass in the front door of Dodge City's Red Light Bordello.

Q. Dealey Plaza in Dallas has become synonymous with the Kennedy assassination, but something significant occurred at that location in the 19th century, as well. What was it?

A. John Neely Bryan built a log cabin overlooking the Trinity River on this site in 1841, first settling what ultimately became Dallas. Construction for flood control and landscaping changed the area somewhat in 1928, and what we know today as Dealey Plaza was built during the Great Depression in a joint project of the Works Progress Administration and the National Youth Administration. In an odd coincidence the Texas Director of the National Youth Administration was Lyndon Johnson, who would later become John F. Kennedy's vice president.

Q. Given the resources that were commonly available on the Nebraska plains in the 1800s, what became a popular source of building materials for new settlers?

A. Sod. There were few trees on the plains, and it was too costly to ship lumber from the East. Pioneers cut blocks of grass and dirt out of the prairie. They used these sod bricks to build houses. Sometimes they just dug under the sod and built cavelike houses.

> ★★★ **FAST FACT** ★★★
>
> During the Gold Rush, one point at the Mississippi River saw 12,000 wagons headed west toward California.

Q. One of the last significant events in the U.S. government's war against Native Americans in the West was the passing of the Dawes Act in 1887. What did the Dawes Act mandate?

A. It converted Native American reservation land into separate parcels. The Dawes Act provided 160 acres for each American Indian family, with the provision that it could not be sold for 25 years. Any extra acreage was sold to pioneers. Although passed with noble intentions, the Dawes Act actually became a continuation of efforts to break up Native American communities and traditions.

SPORTS

★ ★ ★ ★ ★ ★ ★ ★ ★ ★ ★ ★

A lot of sporting events have been held in this country, and a lot of history has been made at them. This chapter reviews some of the more prominent athletic locations in the nation.

Q. What was the site of the first U.S. Olympic Games?

A. St. Louis, Missouri. They were held in conjunction with the Louisiana Purchase Exposition (also known as the St. Louis World's Fair) in 1904.

Q. Why is the Iceland Skating Rink in Paramount, California, important to hockey and figure skating?

A. It is the home of the Zamboni ice-resurfacing machine, which was invented by the rink's owner, Frank Joseph Zamboni Jr. When Zamboni opened his facility in 1939, it took a team of three people up to 90 minutes to repair and resurface the ice after it was gouged by hundreds of skaters. Zamboni built a motorized machine to do the necessary work—sweep, scrape, and saturate—under the operation of just one person. In 1950 three-time Olympic figure skating champion and Hollywood starlet Sonja Henie saw the revolutionary resurfacer at work while rehearsing her new Hollywood Ice Revue at the Iceland. She commissioned Zamboni to build a new model for her upcoming performances in Chicago. That endorsement allowed Zamboni to mass-produce the machines that now bear his name.

Q. What is the oldest continually held sports event in the United States?

A. The Kentucky Derby. This race has been held at Churchill Downs Racetrack in Louisville, Kentucky, since its inception in 1875.

Q. Alaska's annual Iditarod dogsled race was inspired by what remarkable event?

A. Teams of dogsleds carried lifesaving medicine to the site of a deadly diphtheria epidemic in Nome during the winter of 1925. Ships couldn't sail through the frozen sea, planes couldn't fly through the winter storms, and no roads or railroads came close enough to Nome to deliver the supplies. So around 20 teams of sled dogs and mushers hit the Iditarod Trail, relaying medicine 674 miles from Nenana to Nome in not quite 5½ days (a record) and saving many sick children.

Q. What is Major League Baseball's oldest ballpark?

A. Fenway Park in Boston, which opened on April 20, 1912. Although there had been major league ballparks that predated the home of the Boston Red Sox, such as New York's Polo Grounds, Pittsburgh's Forbes Field, and Chicago's Comiskey Park, Fenway is the oldest of baseball's early parks that still stands.

Q. What popular sports drink was developed at the University of Florida?

A. Gatorade. Created in 1965 by UF kidney disease specialist Dr. Robert Cade, the drink is named for the University of Florida Gators.

Q. Why is the Pro Football Hall of Fame located in Canton, Ohio, of all places?

A. Ohio might just lead the NFL in defunct teams. One of these, the Canton Bulldogs (1920–23, 1925–26), won two NFL titles with back-to-back undefeated seasons in 1922 and '23. Leather-helmet nostalgia inspired the Pro Football Hall of Fame to locate in the Bulldogs' old hometown.

TRUE OR FALSE The Harlem Globetrotters basketball team originated in Harlem.

ANSWER False. That just seemed too easy, didn't it? The team started its life in the late 1920s on Chicago's South Side. Manager Abe Saperstein gave them the Harlem designation to highlight the fact that the team was made up of African American players. The Globetrotters didn't actually play their first "home game" in Harlem until 1968.

Q. What was the first race held at the Indianapolis Motor Speedway?

A. The U.S. National Balloon Championship on June 5, 1909. The 2.5-mile oval road racetrack would not be completed for another two months. The first motorcycle race was held there on August 14, 1909, with the first auto race premiering five days later. The site hosted the first Indy 500 race on May 30, 1911.

Q. Wrigley Field is a storied baseball park in Chicago and the world-famous home of the Chicago Cubs. But who built it?

A. Originally named Weeghman Park, Wrigley Field was built in 1914 by Charles Weeghman, a lunchroom operator and owner of the Chicago Whales baseball club of the short-lived Federal League. After that league folded, Weeghman and William Wrigley purchased another team, the Cubs, and moved them from their home at West Side Park to Weeghman's stadium on the north side of town. From 1920 to 1926 it was known as "Cubs Park," but after Wrigley became majority owner of the Cubs in 1926, the park was renamed Wrigley Field.

> *"I'd always thought of Wrigley Field's bleachers as the place where real baseball fans go when they close their eyes and click their heels three times."*
> —Lonnie Wheeler, *Bleachers: A Summer in Wrigley Field*

Q. Where did the "Miracle on Ice" occur?

A. At the 1980 Winter Olympics in Lake Placid, New York. The Soviet Union had dominated international hockey for years, and this event was expected to be no exception. The amateur squad sent to the Olympics by the United States—

The Oldest College Football Bowl Games

★ ★ ★ ★ ★ ★ ★ ★ ★ ★ ★ ★

1. Rose Bowl (1902; it was not played again until 1916 but has been played annually ever since), Pasadena, California
2. Orange Bowl (1935), Miami, Florida
   Sugar Bowl (1935), New Orleans, Louisiana
   Sun Bowl (1935), El Paso, Texas
5. Cotton Bowl (1937), Dallas, Texas

though conditioned and at peak form—was expected to do well but wasn't really considered a contender for the gold medal. Victories over Sweden, Czechoslovakia, Norway, Romania, and West Germany, however, sent Team USA into the medal round against the seemingly invincible Soviets. When the game ended with the Americans winning 4–3 (after trailing 3–2 at the end of the second period), the arena erupted in pandemonium. Sportscaster Al Michaels, who was calling the game on TV, cheered, "Do you believe in miracles? *Yes!*" Team USA needed one more win for the gold medal, and they got it by topping Finland 4–2. The Soviet team took home the silver medal.

Q. Why was Brooklyn's baseball team called "the Dodgers"?

A. Brooklyn fans had to dodge trolleys to get to the ballpark. Washington Park, which was located in the Red Hook area of Brooklyn, served as the home of the Dodgers.

> ★★★ **FAST FACT** ★★★
> Pittsburgh is the only city where all major sports teams have the same colors: black and gold.

Getting to the stadium involved "dodging" the trolley cars of the Brooklyn Rapid Transit Company. In 1913 the Dodgers moved to Ebbets Field in the Brooklyn neighborhood known as Flatbush, but by then the name had stuck.

⭐ Lake Placid, New York, produced three generations of Olympians in one family—the Shea family. Jack Shea (1910-2002) won two gold medals in speed skating at the 1932 Olympics in his hometown; his son Jim competed on the U.S. ski team at the Innsbruck, Austria, games in 1964; and in 2002 grandson Jim Jr. won a gold medal in skeleton at Salt Lake City.

Q. What idea kept athletes in Springfield, Massachusetts, out of the snow in the winter of 1891?

A. Basketball. James Naismith wanted to create a team sport that could be played indoors, out of the cold. He nailed two peach baskets to a railing in the gym, gave the players a large ball, and made up 13 rules.

Q. At which historical baseball field did Babe Ruth hit his famous "called shot"?

A. Wrigley Field, home of the Chicago Cubs. During the 1932 World Series, the Babe pointed to center field to tell the crowd precisely where he intended to pummel the next ball. And then he did. It's much argued among baseball fans as to whether Ruth really called that shot or if he was actually motioning to the Cubs bench or pointing at the pitcher.

Q. Who or what are "The Original Six"?

A. Six NHL hockey teams: the Boston Bruins, New York Rangers, Detroit Red Wings, Chicago Blackhawks, Toronto Maple Leafs, and Montreal Canadiens. However, despite their designation, these are not the first six teams to make up the National Hockey League. Begun in Canada in 1917, the league expanded to include American teams in 1924. In its early years, it featured teams such as the Ottawa Senators, the New York Americans, the Pittsburgh Pirates, the Montreal Maroons, the Hamilton (Ontario) Tigers, and the Philadelphia Quakers. As a result of economic hardship during the Great Depression and losing players to the armed forces in World War II, many of these teams folded, leaving just six still standing. The league remained this way from 1942 until expansion doubled its size in 1967, as six new teams were added to what were now called "The Original Six."

Q. What races make up the U.S. Triple Crown of Thoroughbred Racing, and where are they held?

A. The Kentucky Derby at Churchill Downs in Louisville, Kentucky; the Preakness Stakes at Pimlico Race Course in Baltimore, Maryland; and the Belmont Stakes at Belmont Park in Elmont, New York. In 1919 Sir Barton became the first Triple Crown winner, and ten more horses have won it over the years. The last such horse was Affirmed, which won in 1978.

Q. The village of Cooperstown, New York, was the childhood home of American author James Fenimore Cooper. What else is it known for?

A. The National Baseball Hall of Fame and Museum. In 1905 Albert Spalding, a former baseball player and the founder of Spalding sporting goods, put together a commission to clarify the origins of the sport, which Spalding insisted was an American game. To the surprise of no one, the commission published a report stating exactly that. According to the report, the game had been invented in Cooperstown in 1839 by Abner Doubleday, one of America's 19th-century military heroes. Although the evidence was flimsy and disputed by historians, Spalding and baseball's professional organizations continued to push the myth. In the 1930s a small exhibit of old baseball relics in Cooperstown—including a ball that was supposedly used in Doubleday's first game—proved popular, and Major League Baseball approved the opening of a baseball museum and "hall of fame."

Halls of Fame

★ ★ ★ ★ ★ ★ ★ ★ ★ ★ ★ ★

The Baseball Hall of Fame and Pro Football Hall of Fame have already been discussed, but a number of other sports have halls of fame around the country. Here are a few of them:

- The Naismith Memorial Basketball Hall of Fame, established in 1959, is in Springfield, Massachusetts.

- The World Golf Hall of Fame, established in 1974, has been in St. Augustine, Florida, since 1998.

- The NASCAR Hall of Fame, which opened in 2010, is in Charlotte, North Carolina.

- The National Soccer Hall of Fame, which dates from 1950, is in Oneonta, New York.

- The International Gymnastics Hall of Fame, established in 1986 in Oceanside, California, moved to Oklahoma City, Oklahoma, in 1997.

Q. In 1958, Major League Baseball reached the West Coast as the Brooklyn Dodgers and the New York Giants moved to Los Angeles and San Francisco, respectively. Were these the first two baseball teams to relocate?

A. No, but they were the first to relocate quite so far. In 1902 the Milwaukee Brewers had moved to St. Louis and renamed themselves the Browns; in 1954 they moved again, this time to Baltimore to become the Orioles. In 1903 the original Baltimore Orioles relocated to New York to become the Highlanders (later changing their name to the Yankees). In 1953 the Boston Braves moved to Milwaukee (and would then move to Atlanta in 1966). In 1955 the Philadelphia Athletics relocated to Kansas City (and would then move again to Oakland in 1968).

LANDMARKS, MONUMENTS, AND ATTRACTIONS

★ ★ ★ ★ ★ ★ ★ ★ ★ ★ ★ ★

The United States is full of sites that are immediately recognizable. Natural wonders or the result of human ingenuity, they provoke awe and provide inspiration. How many of these locations can you recognize?

Q. South Dakota's Black Hills are home to what famous patriotic sculpture?

A. Mount Rushmore. Gutzon Borglum was America's most famous sculptor in the 1920s, when he was commissioned to work on this monumental project. Begun in 1927, the work took 14 years and nearly 400 workers to complete. George Washington, Thomas Jefferson, and Abraham Lincoln were obviously subjects for the sculpture, and Theodore Roosevelt, who had held the office of president just 19 years earlier, brought a modern touch to the project.

★ ★ ★ **FAST FACT** ★ ★ ★

Roughly 90 percent of the monument at Mount Rushmore was created by dynamite.

Q. How old is the Golden Gate Bridge?

A. Construction of the bridge began in 1933. The project lasted four years, and the $35-million bridge opened to pedestrian traffic on May 27, 1937, and to vehicles the following day. Upon completion, it was the longest suspension bridge in the world.

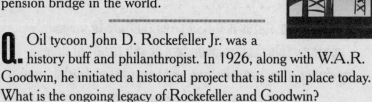

Q. Oil tycoon John D. Rockefeller Jr. was a history buff and philanthropist. In 1926, along with W.A.R. Goodwin, he initiated a historical project that is still in place today. What is the ongoing legacy of Rockefeller and Goodwin?

A. They made Colonial Williamsburg into the world's largest living-history museum. The buildings within the boundaries of the 301-acre site have been painstakingly remodeled and decorated in the styles of prerevolutionary America, while the streets and shops are populated by hired actors who dress in colonial fashion and speak in colonial diction.

The Lincoln Memorial

★ ★ ★ ★ ★ ★ ★ ★ ★ ★ ★ ★

Designed by architect Henry Bacon, sculptor Daniel Chester French, and artist Jules Guerin, the Lincoln Memorial was completed in 1922 to honor the 16th president of the United States. The structure resembles a Greek Doric temple ringed by 36 columns, each representing a state in the Union at the time of Lincoln's death. Seated within the monument is a sculpture of Lincoln, and inscriptions from both the Gettysburg Address and his second inaugural address adorn the south and north walls, respectively. The Lincoln Memorial was the site of Martin Luther King Jr.'s famous "I Have a Dream" speech on August 28, 1963.

TRUE OR FALSE King Kong climbed the World Trade Center in New York City.

ANSWER True. In the 1976 remake starring Jeff Bridges and Jessica Lange, that's exactly what the giant ape did. But that image pales beside the original 1933 film, in which Kong stood atop the Empire State Building with Fay Wray in his hand.

Q. It's been called "America's Front Yard," but by what name is it better known?

A. The National Mall. When architect Pierre L'Enfant laid out his plans for Washington, D.C., in 1790, he envisioned a large, spacious avenue running down the center of the city. But it wasn't until 1851 that architect Andrew Jackson Downing was commissioned to design a landscape plan for the Mall; his plans called for a series of naturalistic parks and gardens with the Washington Monument as its centerpiece. In 1900 a new planning committee headed by Daniel Burnham reimagined the Mall, less as a series of naturalistic parks and more as a geometric open space lined with monuments and federal buildings.

Q. Dealey Plaza in Dallas is well known as the location of the 1963 assassination of John F. Kennedy. According to the official report of the Warren Commission, from where did the shots aimed toward Kennedy's motorcade originate?

A. From the sixth floor of the Texas School Book Depository. Lee Harvey Oswald, a loner and ex-Marine, worked in the building, and he was quickly arrested by police. Oswald himself

Four WPA Achievements Still Used Today

★ ★ ★ ★ ★ ★ ★ ★ ★ ★ ★ ★

During the Great Depression, the U.S. government stepped in to assist the needy and get the economy started again. Perhaps the widest-ranging and most productive New Deal measure was the Works Progress Administration (WPA), which provided more than $10 billion in federal funds from 1935 through the early 1940s and employed millions of people in hundreds of thousands of jobs. Here are the end results of some of the most notable projects that still exist today.

1. Camp David, Maryland: In 1936 the WPA began work on a recreational area in western Maryland's Catoctin Mountains, completing Camp Hi-Catoctin by 1939. For three years it was used as a family camp for federal employees until President Franklin D. Roosevelt visited in April 1942 and selected it as the location for presidential retreats. In the early 1950s President Eisenhower renamed the camp for his grandson.

2. Dealey Plaza, Texas: This park in the heart of Dallas was completed in 1940. Named for an early publisher of the *Dallas Morning News*, the plaza lives in infamy as the location of President John F. Kennedy's assassination on November 22, 1963.

3. LaGuardia Airport, New York: The Big Apple's desire for a city airport was only a dream until September 1937, when the WPA joined with the city to build one. Soon after opening in 1939, it was named New York Municipal Airport-LaGuardia Field to honor mayor Fiorello LaGuardia. The name was shortened to LaGuardia Airport in 1947.

4. Outer Drive Bridge, Illinois: In the heart of the Windy City, this bridge, which crosses the Chicago River near Lake Michigan, was started in 1929, but the Great Depression prevented its completion until the WPA delivered funds in the mid-1930s. When finished in 1937 the bridge was 356 feet long and 100 feet wide, making it the world's longest and widest bascule bridge.

was assassinated just two days later by local nightclub owner Jack Ruby in a police department garage in Dallas.

TRUE OR FALSE Designer John A. Roebling received the key to the city of New York at the opening of his most famous design, the Brooklyn Bridge.

ANSWER False. John A. Roebling did not live to see the 1883 opening of the Brooklyn Bridge. In 1869, while visiting the bridge site before construction began, he was injured, developed tetanus, and died. His son Washington took over the project, but in 1873 he was also injured, suffering the bends while working in pressurized concrete chambers under the river. He became ill and weak, but with the help of his wife, Emily, he directed construction from his home and managed to see the project through.

Willis Tower
★ ★ ★ ★ ★ ★ ★ ★ ★ ★ ★ ★

In 1969 retail giant Sears, Roebuck & Company wanted to consolidate its employees working in offices around the Chicago area. Construction of Chicago's Sears Tower, designed by chief architect Bruce Graham and structural engineer Fazlur Khan of Skidmore, Owings & Merrill, began in 1970. The colossal structure opened in 1973 as the world's tallest building. In 1998 it was surpassed by the Petronas Towers in Malaysia, but it is still the tallest building in the United States. With 110 stories, the distance to the roof is 1,450 feet 7 inches. In 1982 two television antennas were added, increasing its total height to 1,707 feet. To improve broadcast reception, the western antenna was extended in 2000, bringing the total height to 1,725 feet. The Skydeck observatory offers sightseers a view from the 103rd floor, 1,353 feet above the ground. It can be reached in 45 seconds by an express elevator from the lobby. In 2009 Willis Group Holdings leased space in the building and took over the naming rights, officially changing it to Willis Tower.

Q. Hersheypark in Hershey, Pennsylvania, is one of the country's most popular amusement parks, attracting some three million tourists per year. How did it start?

A. It was built in 1907 for the private use of Hershey Chocolate employees. It featured landscaped gardens and lawns and an outdoor theater where vaudevillians performed. Over the next few years Hershey added more theaters, tennis courts, bowling alleys, and even a scenic railroad, while opening the park to the public. In 1912 a specially commissioned carousel was built—which was one of the largest of its kind at the time—and in 1916 a zoo opened, stocked with Hershey founder Milton S. Hershey's personal menagerie. By World War II Hersheypark was one of the prime tourist destinations in Pennsylvania. After Disneyland opened, changing the public's expectation of theme parks, Hersheypark was retooled in 1971.

> ★★★ **FAST FACT** ★★★
> In 2005 an appraisal firm valued Central Park at $528,783,552,000.

Q. Where did 20th-century media mogul William Randolph Hearst build his dazzling 250,000-acre estate?

A. San Simeon, California. Hearst Castle is made up of multiple houses, including the Casa del Mar, the Casa del Monte, the Casa del Sol, and the 60,000-square-foot Casa Grande. The estate also includes the 345,000-gallon outdoor "Neptune Pool," which is surrounded by colonnades, and the smaller indoor "Roman Pool." Famous guests of the castle during Hearst's time included Charlie Chaplin, Winston Churchill, and Franklin Roosevelt. Today the site is managed by the California State Parks department.

Q. As many a parent has said, "Money doesn't grow on trees." So where *does* money come from?

A. Paper money is printed in Washington, D.C., and Fort Worth, Texas, by the Treasury's Bureau of Engraving and Printing. On an average day the bureau prints 26 million notes. Coins are the responsibility of the U.S. Mint, which is also part of the Treasury Department. Circulating coins are stamped in Philadelphia and Denver at a rate of 65 to 80 million per day.

Q. Although this iconic American landmark was first stumbled upon by the Spanish in 1540, significant American exploration of it wasn't undertaken until the 1860s. What site is this?

A. The Grand Canyon. The land that became Arizona was not highly populated earlier in the 19th century, and the canyon itself did not become well known until after the Civil War. John Wesley Powell led the first known expedition down the Colorado

Vietnam Veterans Memorial

★ ★ ★ ★ ★ ★ ★ ★ ★ ★ ★ ★

The Vietnam Veterans Memorial in Washington, D.C., honors the men and women who served in the Vietnam conflict, one of America's most divisive wars. The memorial, which was intended to heal the nation's emotional wounds, was designed to be neutral about the war itself. Three components comprise the memorial: the Wall, with names of soldiers who were killed or missing in action; *The Three Servicemen* statue and flagpole; and the Vietnam Women's Memorial. The Wall was designed by 21-year-old Maya Lin, who submitted the winning sketch, and was built in 1982. Visitors descend a path along two walls of black granite. One wing of the Wall points at the Washington Monument a mile away and the other at the Lincoln Memorial about 600 feet away. When viewed closely, the names of the more than 59,000 killed or missing U.S. soldiers dominate the structure.

River into the canyon in 1869. Almost immediately the government attempted to protect this natural wonder, but miners and ranchers thwarted the effort. It wasn't until 1908 that Teddy Roosevelt declared the canyon a national monument, and in 1919 the Grand Canyon became a national park.

"There is nothing so American as our national parks. The scenery and wildlife are native. The fundamental idea behind the parks is native. It is, in brief, that the country belongs to the people, that it is in process of making for the enrichment of the lives of all of us. The parks stand as the outward symbol of this great human principle."

—Franklin Delano Roosevelt

Q. The Hollywood sign did not start out as a landmark celebrating the movie industry. What was its original purpose?

A. Advertising real estate. In 1923 a real estate developer erected a giant sign reading "Hollywoodland" to advertise the name of a new housing development. It was planned to last for a year and a half, and a few years later the "land" part of the sign fell down and was never replaced.

Q. In 1859 what is perhaps the most famous city park in the country opened. Can you name it?

A. Central Park in New York City. Intended to be a world-class park in a world-class metropolis, the park covers 843 acres in the center of Manhattan. It was designed by Frederick Law Olmsted, and its construction required the transportation of tons of topsoil across the river from New Jersey. Today the park is visited by 25 million people each year.

Q. From 1934 through 1963, it was one of America's most forbidding places, home to a maximum security penitentiary that housed some of America's most notorious criminals, such as Al Capone. What was it?

A. Alcatraz Island in San Francisco Bay. Due to its isolation from the mainland, and the frigid, choppy waters surrounding the island, escape from Alcatraz was nearly impossible; officials claim that in the prison's three-decade history not a single prisoner escaped. This was not for lack of trying: Over the years there were 14 escape attempts from the prison, involving 36 prisoners. The majority of these were recaptured or shot by guards; however, five inmates were never found and are presumed to have drowned.

TRUE OR FALSE Route 66 still thrives today.

ANSWER False. The Interstate Highway System made it obsolete. By 1970 almost every segment of Route 66 had been bypassed by modern four-lane interstate highways. It was officially decommissioned as a federal highway in 1984.

Q. John T. Ford leased and later bought and remodeled First Baptist Church in Washington, D.C. By what name is it better known today?

A. Ford's Theatre. Ford took control of the property in 1861, and by 1863 Ford's Theatre was the premier theatrical venue in Washington, D.C., drawing audiences that included many of the city's dignitaries. President Abraham Lincoln was among these prominent regulars, attending Ford's Theatre more than half a dozen times, mostly to enjoy Shakespearean productions. On April 14, 1865, Lincoln came to see the farce *Our American Cousin*. Midway through the third act, John Wilkes Booth barged into the presidential box and shot Lincoln once behind the left ear. Lincoln died the next morning.

Q. Ellis Island is well known as the port of entry to the United States for immigrants coming from Europe in the early 20th century. Where did immigrants coming from the west enter during that time?

A. Angel Island in San Francisco. From 1910 to 1940 nearly one million people—mostly Chinese and Japanese immigrants—passed through the Angel Island facility. Because of laws such as 1882's "Chinese Exclusion Act," hundreds of thousands of Chinese immigrants were detained in the Angel Island barracks, sometimes for months, while their paperwork was examined. Poems in Chinese characters carved into the walls of the barracks can still be seen by visitors today.

St. Louis Arch

★ ★ ★ ★ ★ ★ ★ ★ ★ ★ ★ ★

The St. Louis Arch on the bank of the Mississippi River marks the city as the "Gateway to the West." Thomas Jefferson's vision of freedom and democracy spreading "from sea to shining sea" inspired architect Eero Saarinen's contemporary design for a 630-foot stainless steel memorial. Construction began in 1963 and was completed on October 28, 1965. The Arch's foundation is set 60 feet into the ground and is built to withstand earthquakes and high winds. A 40-passenger tram takes sightseers from the lobby to the observation platform, where on a clear day the view stretches for 30 miles.

Q. An exodus of bats coming from a hole in the ground in 1901 alerted witnesses to a site that has since become a national park. Where did these bats come from?

A. Carlsbad Caverns in New Mexico. To this day, between 300,000 and 400,000 Brazilian free-tail bats leave in search of food every evening from April to October around twilight.

Q. Today it's the Midwest's top tourist attraction, but when it was first built, it was the largest of its kind in the world. What is it?

A. Navy Pier in Chicago. Originally intended to be a hub for shipping and passenger travel, Municipal Pier, as it was then called, opened in 1916 at the cost of $4.5 million. It featured a series of warehouses, docking areas, and passenger terminals for ferries to and from the city. With the coming of World War I, however, it proved an excellent location to house regiments of naval personnel, as well as Red Cross offices and home defense units. At the end of the war, the pier returned to civilian use. Its name was changed to Navy Pier in 1927.

Q. What tremendous feat of engineering altered the flow of the Colorado River in Nevada?

A. Hoover Dam. Construction was initiated in 1931. Workers lived in dismal camps and endured brutal working conditions and searing temperatures that caused a total of almost 100 worker fatalities. Besides these official fatalities, dozens more workers died of what the construction company called "pneumonia" but what was later determined to be carbon-monoxide poisoning from using unsafe machinery

Empire State Building

★ ★ ★ ★ ★ ★ ★ ★ ★ ★ ★ ★ ★

The Empire State Building is the crown jewel of the New York City skyline. Designed by William Lamb, the art deco structure was the world's tallest building when it opened in 1931, soaring 1,454 feet from the ground to the top of its lightning rod. More than 3,000 workers took less than 14 months to build the structure, with the framework erected at a pace of 4.5 stories per week. Today, visitors still marvel at the breathtaking views visible from the observatory, which on a clear day offers glimpses of the five surrounding states.

in unventilated tunnels. Despite this, the dam was finished in five years—two years ahead of schedule. Initially christened Boulder Dam, the name was later changed to Hoover Dam to honor Herbert Hoover, who was president when construction began and who helped coordinate the project.

Q. What memorial project was conceived by Native Americans as a response to Mount Rushmore?

A. The Crazy Horse Memorial. Also in the Black Hills of South Dakota, roughly 17 miles from the four presidents, this memorial dwarfs Rushmore in size. Lakota Sioux chief Henry Standing Bear famously stated, "My fellow chiefs and I would like the white man to know that the red man has great heroes, also." Korczak Ziolkowski, a Polish American sculptor who had worked on Mount Rushmore, agreed to take on the project in 1948. When finished, the memorial is to measure 641 feet long by 563 feet high. So far, only the head has been completed, but work continues.

Q. What was the name of Liberty Island before the Statue of Liberty was erected there?

Eleven Facts About the Statue of Liberty

★ ★ ★ ★ ★ ★ ★ ★ ★ ★ ★ ★

1. The statue's real name is "Liberty Enlightening the World."

2. Lady Liberty was sculpted by Frédéric Auguste Bartholdi; Alexandre Gustave Eiffel was the structural engineer.

3. Construction of the statue began in France in 1875. It was completed in Paris in June 1884, given to the American people on July 4, 1884, and reassembled and dedicated in the United States on October 28, 1886.

4. The model for the face of the statue is reputed to be the sculptor's mother, Charlotte Bartholdi.

5. The inscription on the statue's tablet reads: July 4, 1776 (in Roman numerals).

6. More than four million people visit the Statue of Liberty each year.

7. Symbolizing freedom and the opportunity for a better life, the Statue of Liberty greeted millions of immigrants as they sailed through New York Harbor on their way to nearby Ellis Island.

8. Lady Liberty is 152 feet 2 inches tall from base to torch and 305 feet 1 inch tall from the ground to the tip of her torch.

9. There are 192 steps from the ground to the top of the pedestal and 354 steps from the pedestal to the crown.

10. Lady Liberty's sandals are 25 feet long, making her shoe size 879.

11. The statue functioned as an actual lighthouse from 1886 to 1902. There was an electric plant on the island to generate power for the light, which could be seen 24 miles away.

A. Bedloe's Island. As a matter of fact, it kept that name until President Eisenhower approved the change to Liberty Island in 1956.

Washington Monument

★ ★ ★ ★ ★ ★ ★ ★ ★ ★ ★

The Washington Monument, a 555-foot-high white obelisk situated at the west end of the National Mall in Washington, D.C., honors George Washington. Comprised of 36,491 marble, granite, and sandstone blocks, the structure was designed by prominent American architect Robert Mills. Construction began in 1848, but due to the outbreak of the Civil War and lack of funding, it took nearly 40 years to complete. The clearly visible difference in the marble's shading about 150 feet up the obelisk marks the point where work resumed in 1876. The monument was dedicated in 1885—on Washington's Birthday, February 22— but it didn't officially open to the public until October 9, 1888, after internal construction was complete. At the time it was the world's tallest structure, but this was a title it held only until 1889, when the Eiffel Tower was completed in Paris.

Q. Where is the Barringer Crater and how was it created?

A. Arizona. Around 50,000 years ago, a 160-foot meteorite landed in the northern desert, leaving an impact crater about a mile wide and 570 feet deep. Scientists believe the meteorite that caused the crater was traveling roughly 28,600 miles per hour when it struck Earth, causing an explosion as much as 150 times more powerful than the Hiroshima atomic bomb. The meteorite itself probably melted in the explosion, spreading a mist of molten nickel and iron across the surrounding landscape. The Barringer Crater—or Meteor Crater, as it is more commonly known—is a popular tourist attraction.

BUSINESS AND INDUSTRY

★ ★ ★ ★ ★ ★ ★ ★ ★ ★ ★ ★

Much of America's success on the world stage has been built on its industrial strength and business acumen. Over the years the dollars and cents added up, and the nation needed a thriving finance sector to count it all. Find out if your knowledge of places of business is "right on the money."

Q. If there's a single place that defines business in America, it must be Wall Street in New York City. How did Wall Street get its name?

A. There used to be an actual wall there. The narrow street in lower Manhattan that is the center of the U.S. financial world takes its name from a wall built by Dutch colonists in 1653 to defend the city against an expected attack by Native Americans. The British took the wall down in 1699.

Q. An energy crisis in the 1840s forced up prices of a common fuel that was central to the industry of New England. What was this fuel?

A. Whale oil. In the 1840s whale oil was burned for light and was useful for the lubrication of machines. By the 1850s, despite a whaling fleet of more than 700 vessels in New England's ports, prices had leapt to two dollars a gallon. Americans started looking for alternatives, such as coal oil and petroleum.

★ In 1865, Cincinnati's Commercial Hospital became the first U.S. hospital to provide ambulance service. James A. Jackson was paid $360 a year as the first recorded ambulance driver. Before this, those needing hospital care had to get there on their own. Bellevue Hospital in New York started a similar service in 1869.

TRUE OR FALSE In Detroit, Michigan, Henry Ford developed the first industrial assembly line used in America.

ANSWER False. Ford may have streamlined the process, but the assembly line first saw use in a Cincinnati, Ohio, slaughter-house. Cincinnati was the center of pork production in the 1850s, and a highly organized system of moving pig carcasses was developed there. In 1860 Wilson, Eggleston & Company installed an overhead track that sped up the process and made history.

Q. Where was the nation's first oil well drilled?

A. Near Titusville, Pennsylvania, in 1859. Crude oil had long been used in small quantities in the places where it happened to seep from underground, but Titusville made oil extraction big business. Pennsylvania looked like it had a successful industry on its hands.

Q. The United Auto Workers union (UAW) was organized in 1935, but General Motors refused to recognize the organization. Where did workers take a stand to force GM to accept the union?

A. Flint, Michigan. Though maybe "take a stand" is the wrong choice of words. When workers in Flint heard rumors that GM was going to move work to factories where the union was weaker, they held a sit-down strike. Instead of leaving the factory and picketing, which would have allowed GM to bring in other workers, the union members stayed in their normal workplaces and just sat there. The union's Women's Auxiliary took up picketing outside, organized a first-aid station, provided child care, and collected food and money for strikers and their families. On March 12, 1937, General Motors agreed to recognize the UAW, and the strike ended.

Q. More than 600 banks failed each year between 1921 and 1929, but because they were mostly small, rural banks, the government was not concerned with passing bank insurance legislation. On December 11, 1930, however, another bank closed and made the issue a greater priority. What was the important bank that went under?

A. The Bank of the United States in New York City. When the Bank of the United States closed, it wiped out the savings of nearly half a million people. Another 2,300 banks went out of business in 1931 with no insurance to protect their customers.

> *"Wall Street is the only place that people ride to in a Rolls Royce to get advice from those who take the subway."*
> —Warren Buffett

⭐ Immediately after the stock market collapse of October 1929, the prestigious *Harvard Economic Society Weekly Letter* predicted that a severe depression was outside the range of probability. In its issue for November 15, 1930, the *Weekly Letter* predicted "the end of the decline in business during the early part of 1931 and steady…revival for the remainder of the year." They continued to expect the economy to turn the corner, but their money ran out before it did. The *Weekly Letter* stopped publication in 1931.

Q. The first building to be called a *skyscraper* was erected in Chicago by the Home Insurance Company of New York. Construction began on May 1, 1884, and took a little more than a year to complete. How tall was it?

A. Ten stories. The Home Insurance building, which contained nine floors and a basement, was made of a steel frame supporting marble walls. Two stories were later added for a grand total of 12. By comparison, the Willis Tower (formerly known as the Sears Tower) in Chicago, which opened in 1973, has 110 stories.

Q. How did the Walt Disney Company control what businesses could open in the area around Walt Disney World in Orlando, Florida?

A. It bought about 27,000 acres of land around the area. Walt Disney had been disappointed in how the area around Disneyland in California had been developed, so he made sure that he and his company would have a voice in what was built around the Florida theme park. Although Disney died in 1966, his brother Roy Disney saw the project through to fruition. Walt Disney World, consisting at the time of only the Magic Kingdom and two hotels, opened to the public in 1971.

Q. In 1970 this area in Northern California was still called Valley of the Heart's Delight. By what name is it better known today?

A. Silicon Valley. The original name was inspired by fertile orchards that had once made this an agricultural area. Silicon Valley began when William Shockley, a scientist who had led the team that developed the transistor at Bell Labs in New Jersey, decided that he wanted to manufacture transistors out of silicon in his own lab near his hometown of Palo Alto. Although Shockley's firm eventually failed, the scientific talent he had assembled went on to create the framework that anchored Silicon Valley's phenomenal success.

Q. When and where was the Buttonwood Agreement signed?

A. In 1792 under a buttonwood tree near Wall Street. After a financial panic, a bank bailout of sorts, and the jailing of at least one investor, 24 brokers and dealers came together and signed an agreement to fix their commission prices and to favor each other over anyone who didn't sign, forming what was basically a business club (or, in a more sinister term, a cartel). In 1817 this group evolved into a more formal organization: the New York Stock and Exchange Board. They streamlined their name to the New York Stock Exchange in 1863 and continued to fix the price of commissions until 1975.

Q. Texas is known for its oil wells, but it wasn't always that way. Where was the first major gusher struck that kicked off the Texas Oil Boom?

A. Spindletop. This was in southeast Texas near Beaumont. The first strike there in 1901 wasn't an ordinary well: It was a 15-story gusher that initially produced more oil than all the

The Top-Producing Oil Fields in Texas

★ ★ ★ ★ ★ ★ ★ ★ ★ ★ ★ ★

Texas currently has 5 billion barrels of known petroleum deposits, which is about a quarter of the known reserves in the United States, although the actual total size and volume of individual reserves are often kept secret by the companies removing the oil. These are the top ten largest Texas oil fields ranked by proven reserves estimated from recent data. Included in this list are the year each field was discovered and its size in acreage (when known).

1. Wasson Field, West Texas. Discovered in 1937, covers 62,500 acres

2. Spraberry Trend, West Texas. Discovered in 1949, covers 500,000 acres

3. Slaughter, West Texas. Discovered in 1937, covers 100,000 acres

4. Levelland, West Texas. Discovered in 1945

5. Seminole, West Texas. Discovered in 1936

6. Goldsmith, West Texas. Discovered in 1935

7. Yates, Southwest Texas. Discovered in 1926, covers 22,500 acres

8. Cowden North, West Texas. Discovered in 1930

9. Giddings, South central Texas. Discovered in 1960

10. Kelly-Snyder, West Texas. Discovered in 1948

other wells in the country put together. As recently as 1983 more than a quarter of the state's tax revenue came from the oil and gas industry.

▬▬▬▬▬▬▬▬▬▬▬▬▬▬▬▬▬▬▬▬▬▬▬▬▬

Q. Wine is produced in various places around the United States, but what is considered the nation's premier wine-growing region?

A. The Napa Valley in California. Its viticultural history began in 1836 with George Calvert Yount, an early settler who planted the region's first vineyards. By 1860 other grape growers had arrived, and in 1861 the first commercial vineyard was established by Charles Krug. By the late 19th century more than 140 vineyards were operating in the region. The area had its ups and downs over the next several years, but it was resuscitated in the mid-1960s when Robert Mondavi opened the first modern vineyard in the area. In 1999 Napa Valley was named one of nine "Great Wine Capitals" around the world.

Q. In the fall of 1930 more than 6,000 people were peddling a product on the street corners of New York City that went on to become a memorable symbol of the Great Depression. What were they selling?

A. Apples. That year the International Apple Shippers Association discovered it had a surplus of unsold fruit, so it offered the apples on credit to those who were out of work. The apple peddlers sold them for five cents each.

Q. What 1859 discovery of silver on the east side of the Sierra Nevada Mountains effectively signaled the end of the California Gold Rush?

A. The Comstock Lode. When word spread of the fabulously rich silver deposit that was found in the territory that was to become Nevada, the area

★★★ **FAST FACT** ★★★

The Baltimore and Ohio Railroad started the first passenger train service in America in 1830. The steam-powered locomotive ran for 13 miles in Maryland between Baltimore and the town of Ellicott's Mills, chugging along at a top speed of 20 miles per hour.

quickly attracted large numbers of discouraged prospectors from the other side of the mountains. Those prospectors remained discouraged. The simple, ancient techniques they'd used to pan for gold were completely unsuited for silver mining. Silver mining required expertise and capital to tunnel deep enough into the earth to extract the precious metal. Instead, these spoils went to the mining barons.

Q. What vegetable-based toy started an empire in Rhode Island?

A. Mr. Potato Head. In the late 1940s George Lerner had the idea to create plastic mouths, eyes, and noses that could be pushed into pieces of produce to make funny faces. Toy companies dismissed the idea, but in 1951 Lerner met with Rhode Island toymakers Hassenfeld Brothers, a small family-owned company that sold school supplies and was trying to move into the toy market. The Hassenfelds loved Lerner's idea, and on April 30, 1952, the Mr. Potato Head Funny Face kit debuted, selling for just under a dollar. As the first toy advertised on TV, it became an instant success, with sales hitting more than $4 million in the first year. That gave Hassenfeld Brothers the leg up that the firm needed to break into the toy market. Company officials also streamlined the company name to better suit their new image, rebranding themselves as Hasbro.

THE CIVIL WAR

★ ★ ★ ★ ★ ★ ★ ★ ★ ★ ★ ★

It was a period of the nation's past that pitted "brother against brother." These places from Yankee territory and across the Mason-Dixon Line to the Deep South are among the most well known in all of American history. What's your Civil War IQ?

Q. Where were the first shots of the Civil War fired?

A. Charleston, South Carolina. At 4:30 A.M. on April 12, 1861, Confederate artillery began shelling Fort Sumter in Charleston Harbor. As a bastion that was well designed to repel a sea attack, Sumter and its artillery weren't prepared to defend themselves from land-based rebel batteries. At 2:30 P.M. on April 14, Union Major Robert Anderson surrendered his fortress to the Confederacy.

Q. How many states had seceded from the Union by the time hostilities broke out?

A. Seven. South Carolina had led off the exodus on December 20, 1860. Mississippi, Florida, Alabama, Georgia, and Louisiana followed suit in January of the next year, with Texas joining on February 1. Virginia left the Union three days after the April 14 fall of Fort Sumter, and Arkansas and North Carolina withdrew in May. Tennessee was the last state to pull out of the Union, leaving on June 8, 1861.

TRUE OR FALSE The Bluegrass state of Kentucky was part of the Confederacy.

ANSWER False. After South Carolina seceded from the Union in December 1860, Kentucky declared itself a neutral state in the burgeoning conflict—the governor

wanted to secede, but the legislature was staunchly Unionist. In September 1861, however, the border state aligned itself with the North. Kentucky was one of four states (along with Maryland, Delaware, and Missouri) that did not join the Confederacy even though citizens in those states could legally own slaves.

Q. Much of the fighting during the Civil War was limited to Southern territory, but Confederate forces made some successful excursions north. What was the northernmost U.S. city to be attacked by Confederate forces?

A. St. Albans, Vermont. In early October 1864 several men checked into a hotel in sleepy St. Albans, located just 15 miles south of the Canadian border. On each of the next few days, two or three more men joined them until there were about 20 in all. They were a friendly group, at least until October 19 when the group simultaneously robbed three area banks. The plan was executed with the full knowledge of the Confederate government, and the money was intended to go into rebel coffers. The raiders escaped over the border only to be captured by Canadian police.

★ Washington, D.C., which is located on the Potomac River between Maryland and Virginia, is a fair distance south of the Mason-Dixon Line. In 1864 Confederate troops came within

30 miles of mounting an attack on the nation's capital. Desperate to offset attacks on Southern cities by Union Generals Ulysses S. Grant and William Tecumseh Sherman, Confederate General Robert E. Lee sent General Jubal Early to strike the U.S. capital. With the Capitol dome in view, the Confederate general was turned away by Union troops led by General Lew Wallace. It may have been a case of Early being too late.

Q. What was the name of the Civil War's most infamous prisoner-of-war camp?

A. Andersonville. The Andersonville stockade in the heart of Georgia was built to house fewer than 10,000 Union prisoners, but by August 1864, more than 33,000 POWs were crammed in under terrible conditions. Nearly 13,000 soldiers died of disease, poor sanitation, malnutrition, or exposure to the elements. Andersonville was one of many POW camps, but its commander, Captain Henry Wirz, was the only soldier executed for his actions during the war.

Q. Where is Confederate General Thomas "Stonewall" Jackson buried?

A. This is a bit of a trick question. Most of him is buried at Virginia Military Institute in Lexington, Virginia, where he was a professor for a number of years before the Civil War. His left arm, however, is buried near where it was amputated after the Battle of Chancellorsville.

Q. Which U.S. state was formed as a direct result of the Confederacy's secession from the Union?

A. West Virginia. This region was part of Virginia when that state left the Union in 1861. But many in the western counties were already unhappy with their leaders in Richmond and took the opportunity to break free. West Virginia seceded from Virginia and gained admittance to the United States on April 20, 1863.

TRUE OR FALSE Arlington Cemetery was once the site of Robert E. Lee's home.

ANSWER True. Arlington was originally owned by George Washington Parke Custis, who intended it to be a living memorial to his adopted grandfather, George Washington. After Custis's death in 1857, the property passed to his daughter, who had married Robert E. Lee in 1831. Early in the war, Lee and his wife abandoned the estate, which later became a Union

The Union States
★ ★ ★ ★ ★ ★ ★ ★ ★ ★ ★ ★

1. California
2. Connecticut
3. Delaware
4. Illinois
5. Indiana
6. Iowa
7. Kansas
8. Kentucky
9. Maine
10. Maryland
11. Massachusetts
12. Michigan
13. Minnesota
14. Missouri
15. Nevada (admitted in 1864)
16. New Hampshire
17. New Jersey
18. New York
19. Ohio
20. Oregon
21. Pennsylvania
22. Rhode Island
23. Vermont
24. West Virginia (admitted in 1863)
25. Wisconsin

Army headquarters. During the war, 200 acres were set aside for a cemetery for Union troops.

Q. Some of Abraham Lincoln's most famous words were: "Fourscore and seven years ago." Where did he speak them?

A. Gettysburg, Pennsylvania. He was dedicating a new military cemetery in November 1863, four months after the Northern army had stopped General Robert E. Lee's furthest incursion into Union territory. Fourscore and seven equals 87, so Lincoln was referring to the number of years that had passed since the signing of the Declaration of Independence.

Q. How long was Lincoln's Gettysburg Address?

A. Just two minutes. The entire text was under 300 words. Lincoln followed a popular orator named Edward Everett, who had just delivered a two-hour-long speech. The day after they each spoke, Everett wrote to Lincoln: "I should be glad, if I could flatter myself that I came as near to the central idea of the occasion, in two hours, as you did in two minutes."

Q. Although many may not be happy with the name today, by what nickname was the Kansas Territory known before it became a state?

A. Bloody Kansas. In 1854 the Kansas-Nebraska Act established the territories of Kansas and Nebraska and withdrew the prohibition against slavery set in those areas by the Missouri Compromise of 1820. The state of Missouri began a strong-arm campaign in Kansas, encouraging proslavery settlers to pour in, rigging local elections, and bullying abolitionists. Antislavery forces supported their Kansas frontliners with shipments of weapons. A continuous, undeclared, bloody border skirmish along the Kansas-Nebraska border lasted for several years and into the Civil War, gaining Kansas its gory nickname.

> **★★★ FAST FACT ★★★**
>
> The Shenandoah Valley town of Winchester, Virginia, was the site of several major Civil War battles. It changed hands 70 times over the course of the war.

Q. What infamous slave was born in 1800 in Southampton County, Virginia?

A. Nat Turner. In August 1831 he led a slave rebellion that moved from house to house in Southampton County, murdering white men, women, and children. Newly liberated slaves joined the rebellion, which grew to about 40 mounted rebels. By the middle of the second day, however, a white militia stopped the rebels, leaving a final toll of about 60 white people dead. Turner eluded capture for more than two months, but on November 11, 1831, he was executed.

Q. Where did the Lincoln-Douglas debates take place?

A. In Illinois. Abraham Lincoln ran for president in 1860 against Stephen A. Douglas, John C. Breckinridge, and John Bell, and many people mistakenly believe that the Lincoln-Douglas debates took place at that time. This isn't the case. Two years earlier, Lincoln and Douglas had faced each other in a race for a Senate seat in Illinois, and this was the setting for the celebrated contests. Facing off against the incumbent Douglas, Lincoln challenged his opponent to a debate in each of Illinois's nine congressional districts. The format they followed was not one we'd recognize today: It allowed 60 minutes for the opening speaker, 90 minutes for rebuttal, and 30 more for the opening speaker's rejoinder. After it was all over, Douglas was reelected to the Senate.

Q. Where did the Civil War end?

A. Appomattox Court House, Virginia. On April 9, 1865, Ulysses S. Grant accepted Robert E. Lee's surrender in the town of Appomattox Court House in the south-central part of the state. The Confederate capital of Richmond, Virginia, had already fallen a few days
earlier, and although there were still other armies fighting in the field, Lee's surrender essentially put an end to the war.

Q. What was Wilmer McLean's connection to the beginning and the end of the Civil War?

A. The war began in his kitchen and finished in his parlor. McLean owned a home in Manassas, Virginia—a house that Confederate General P.G.T. Beauregard took over as his headquarters during the First Battle of Bull Run, the war's first major confrontation. The battle was essentially fought in McLean's yard. Beauregard later wrote that a cannonball landed in the kitchen while he and his staff were having dinner. For various reasons—the health and welfare of his family likely primary among them—McLean left Manassas to move further west. He settled in Appomattox Court House where, on April 9, 1865, soldiers came knocking at his door to use his parlor for a meeting of Generals Lee and Grant.

> *"I beg to present you as a Christmas gift the city of Savannah."*
>
> —General William Sherman to President Lincoln on December 22, 1864, after Sherman's march to the sea

Q. What was the bloodiest single-day battle in American history?

A. Antietam. On September 17, 1862, more than a year after the Civil War had begun, Union General Joseph Hooker faced Confederate General Robert E. Lee near Sharpsburg, Maryland. The day's fighting was brutal and severe, and by

The Confederate States

★ ★ ★ ★ ★ ★ ★ ★ ★ ★ ★

State	Date of Secession
1. South Carolina	December 20, 1860
2. Mississippi	January 9, 1861
3. Florida	January 10, 1861
4. Alabama	January 11, 1861
5. Georgia	January 19, 1861
6. Louisiana	January 26, 1861
7. Texas	February 1, 1861
8. Virginia	April 17, 1861
9. Arkansas	May 6, 1861
10. North Carolina	May 20, 1861
11. Tennessee	June 8, 1861

nightfall, the dead lay in heaps all around Sharpsburg. All in all, more than 23,000 soldiers were killed or wounded in the battle, which essentially resulted in a draw.

Q. How far west did fighting in the Civil War extend?

A. The Battle of Picacho Pass is considered the westernmost battle of the Civil War. It was fought between members of the California Column—Union soldiers based out of Camp Drum—and Confederates from Texas at a site located between modern-day

> **★★★ FAST FACT ★★★**
>
> While the Civil War brought many parts of the nation terrible economic hardship, Chicago's population and industry tripled from 1861 to '70. It sure helps to be far away from the fighting!

Tucson and Phoenix, Arizona. Marching east from Wilmington, California, to secure control of the New Mexico territory, the Union soldiers fought the Confederates to a draw, losing three of their own.

Q. Where did the last recorded shipment of slaves from Africa to the United States land?

A. Mobile, Alabama. Although U.S. law prohibited the importation of slaves into the country starting in 1808, the last known shipment of smuggled African slaves arrived in Mobile Bay in July 1860. Reportedly as a result of a bet, shipper Timothy Meaher sent his ship *Cotilde* (or *Cotilda*) to Africa; it returned with a cargo of more than 100 slaves. Although Meaher was apprehended and prosecuted for the crime, Alabama's secession from the Union made federal prosecution impossible, and charges were dismissed.

Q. What was the name of the town where General Lee's northern momentum was stopped in the summer of 1863?

A. Gettysburg, Pennsylvania. Lee had been attempting to bring the war to Northern territory and was heading in the direction of Pennsylvania's capital, Harrisburg. Hearing that a division of Union cavalry was near the crossroads town of Gettysburg, Lee thought it a good idea to test Union strength. It wasn't. After three days of fighting and 50,000 casualties on both sides, Lee retreated back toward the Mason-Dixon Line.

Q. Which state had dueling Union and Confederate governments during the Civil War?

A. Arkansas. The state seceded from the Union to join the Confederacy, but when the Union Army took over northern Arkansas in 1863, Arkansas Confederates abandoned the state capital in Little Rock and formed a new one in the southwestern Arkansas town of Washington. The occupying Union Army, however, established a governor and continued to consider Little Rock the capital. Both capitals remained until the end of the war.

Q. After Abraham Lincoln died, where did the funeral train go on its way to its final destination of Springfield, Illinois?

A. It took almost three weeks to travel the scenic route across the country so that a large number of citizens could come out to pay their respects. The train stopped in Baltimore, Maryland; Harrisburg and Philadelphia, Pennsylvania; New York City, Albany, and Buffalo, New York; Cleveland and Columbus, Ohio; Indianapolis, Indiana; and Chicago, Illinois. It traveled through hundreds of smaller towns and train stations along the way, retracing—in reverse—the route Lincoln took from Springfield to D.C. after winning the presidency.

POLITICS

★ ★ ★ ★ ★ ★ ★ ★ ★ ★ ★ ★

Although civic officials might want to think differently, American government runs on politics. The ebb and flow of power, the expansion of civil rights—it all comes down to the political struggle. Test your knowledge about these places of political significance.

Q. Which was the first state to give women the right to vote and hold office?

A. Wyoming, although it was still a territory at the time. Wyoming has a number of female firsts: The legislature passed a law allowing women to vote in 1869. As a result, Esther Morris became the nation's first female judge in 1870. Wyoming also elected the nation's first woman governor, Nellie Tayloe Ross, in 1925.

Q. Rosa Parks refused to give up her seat on a bus in what Southern city?

A. Montgomery, Alabama. On December 1, 1955, Parks, a 42-year-old African American woman, was taking the bus home from work when she deliberately broke the state's segregation law by refusing to turn over her seat to a standing white passenger. Parks was arrested and was later found guilty, being punished with a suspended sentence and a fine. Her action set off a successful, yearlong boycott of the Montgomery bus system by the black community led by a young preacher named Martin Luther King Jr. Many people consider this event to be the beginning of the modern U.S. Civil Rights movement.

Q. Where did the Republican Party begin?

A. A number of towns claim to be the birthplace of the Republican Party. Exeter, New Hampshire, has the earliest claim, pointing to a meeting of abolitionists called by Amos Tuck in 1853 at Major Blake's Hotel (aka the Squamscott Hotel) in which the formation of an anti-slavery "Republican Party" was discussed. Unfortunately, no action seems to have been taken following this meeting, and the Republican Party wasn't officially established in New Hampshire for another few years. Crawfordsville, Iowa, takes the next claim chronologically, arguing that defectors from the Whig Party met in private at Seceder Church there in February 1854 to plan a new party. A month after that, what is sometimes considered the first public meeting of proto-Republicans was held at the Little White Schoolhouse in Ripon, Wisconsin. Finally, the first official party meeting, a statewide convention that created a party platform and nominated candidates for office, took place outdoors in Jackson, Michigan, on July 6, 1854.

Q. On May 4, 1970, protesting university students started throwing rocks at National Guard troops. The confrontation culminated with the troops firing on the students. Where did this happen?

A. Kent State University in Ohio. Tension had been mounting for several days as students reacted to the news of U.S. troops invading Cambodia. The situation escalated further on May 4 when troops using tear gas and advancing with fixed bayonets slowed but failed to end the protest. At 12:24 P.M., a National Guard sergeant fired his .45 pistol. At least two dozen soldiers followed suit, firing more than 60 shots. The 13-second volley killed two protestors and two uninvolved students while wounding nine. Only two of those hit were within 50 yards of the National Guard. Protests, often enormous and sometimes violent, soon wracked college campuses and major cities around the nation. None of the troops involved in the Kent State incident was prosecuted; the legal system accepted the defense that they feared for their lives.

Q. The Missouri Compromise proved very fortunate for which New England state?

A. Maine. In 1820 Maine was part of Massachusetts, and slavery was a preeminent issue in the Unites States. The nation had 22 states, 11 that allowed slavery and 11 that did not. Neither side wanted the other to have more member states, but Missouri, a slave territory, was seeking statehood. As part of what came to be called the Missouri Compromise, Maine joined the Union as a free state at the same time Missouri was admitted as a slave state. In this way, the number of states allowing slaves and the number prohibiting them remained equal.

Q. A significant event in modern Native American activism occurred in 1969 when American Indians began a 19-month occupation of what American landmark?

A. Alcatraz. Native Americans arrived on the island on November 20, 1969, and remained there until June 11, 1971. The occupiers felt that, in line with past treaties, any government land that was not being used—such as Alcatraz—should be returned to the tribes. This event put a national spotlight on the issue of Native American rights and resulted in new federal legislation supporting self-determination for Native American peoples.

<hr>

Q. Wyoming was the first state to give women the vote. Which was the second?

A. Utah, in 1870 when it was still a territory. The movement originated out of state and was hardly motivated by altruistic concern for women's political rights. Its supporters believed Utah's women would dispense with polygamy if given the vote. The plan backfired on two levels: Not only did senior male Mormon leaders support it, but most Mormon women voters continued to vote for polygamy. The gambit having bombed, the U.S. Congress canceled woman suffrage in Utah in 1887. Women got it back in 1895.

<hr>

Q. Where is the Edmund Pettus Bridge, and why is it significant?

A. Selma, Alabama. It was the site of three civil rights marches in March 1965. The first, on March 7, was to protest the murder of unarmed civil rights protestor Jimmie Lee Jackson by an Alabama state trooper during a peaceful demonstration the previous month. Marchers intended to walk to Alabama's state capital, Montgomery, but they could barely get across the bridge. Instead, the peaceful, unarmed

marchers were savagely attacked by state troopers with billy clubs and tear gas. The ABC TV network interrupted its national programming to televise live footage of the violence. The resulting national outcry over the brutal police actions led to two larger marches over the next two weeks, both led by Dr. Martin Luther King Jr. The last of them, on March 21, ultimately saw nearly 25,000 people march into Montgomery.

TRUE OR FALSE Martin Luther King Jr. was assassinated while giving a speech in Washington, D.C.

ANSWER False. King was shot the evening of April 4, 1968, while standing on the balcony outside his room at the Lorraine Motel in Memphis, Tennessee, where he had traveled to support striking African American sanitation workers. James Earl Ray was later captured and charged with the crime. He confessed to the assassination but recanted a few days later.

> ★★★ **FAST FACT** ★★★
>
> The Lorraine Motel is now the National Civil Rights Museum.

Q. On June 17, 1972, five men were arrested while in the process of breaking into offices inside this office complex in Washington, D.C., an event that proved to have widespread consequences. What was the name of the office complex?

A. Watergate. The five burglars were entering the headquarters of the Democratic National Committee. They had ties to both the CIA and the Republican Party, and three of them were Cuban nationals. The break-in was eventually tied to President Richard Nixon and his top aides, and the resulting Watergate scandal and Congressional hearings led to Nixon's resignation.

> *"Washington is a city of Southern efficiency and Northern charm."*
> —John F. Kennedy

Seven Memorials on the National Mall

* * * * * * * * * * * *

The National Mall in Washington, D.C., is truly a national treasure. On the east side is the Capitol, with the National Gallery of Art to the north. Museums of the Smithsonian Institution dot the landscape, and the Washington Monument is almost right in the middle. Here are seven memorials that should be part of any walking tour:

1. World War II Memorial
2. Vietnam Veterans Memorial
3. Lincoln Memorial
4. Korean War Veterans Memorial
5. Martin Luther King, Jr. Memorial
6. Franklin Delano Roosevelt Memorial
7. Thomas Jefferson Memorial

Q. In 1886 protesting for an eight-hour workday was a hot issue. Where did it come to a boil?

A. Haymarket Square in Chicago. More than 35,000 workers walked off the job on May 1, and when the strike continued to grow, crowds gathered and harassed the police, who responded with gunfire. Several strikers were killed. A gathering in Haymarket Square protested the killings. The police presence was heavy, and when police ordered protesters to disperse, someone threw a bomb, killing one officer instantly and wounding many others. Police began firing into the crowd, and a brawl broke out. Several officers and protesters were killed; many more were injured. Police arrested hundreds in the Haymarket Riot but couldn't find the bomb thrower. In desperation, prosecutors charged eight prominent anarchists with murder. Offering no bombing evidence, the prosecution used the anarchists' pamphlets and speeches to convict them of conspiracy. All eight were found guilty—four were hanged, and one committed suicide in jail. The three remaining prisoners were pardoned by the Illinois governor in 1893.

Q. In 1954 the U.S. Supreme Court ruled that "separate but equal" statutes segregating blacks and whites in virtually every avenue of public life were not constitutional. The case leading to this decision is informally referred to as *Brown v. Board of Education*. Where was that board of education?

A. Topeka, Kansas. Oliver L. Brown headed the group of plaintiffs, 13 African American Topeka parents acting on behalf of their children. Brown's daughter Linda, a third grader, had to walk six blocks and through a railyard to catch a bus to a segregated school a mile away. The nearest white school was only seven blocks away. Charles Hamilton Houston and Thurgood Marshall, who together headed the NAACP legal department, represented the plaintiffs.

Q. The 19th Amendment to the U.S. Constitution guarantees American women the right to vote. It was passed by the House of Representatives on May 21, 1919, and by the Senate on June 4. With a total of 48 states in the Union at the time, 36 were needed to ratify the amendment and change the Constitution. Which was the 36th state to ratify?

A. Tennessee. Illinois, Michigan, and Wisconsin ratified the amendment within a week of Congress passing it, but the 36th ratification didn't occur until August 18, 1920, more than a year later. The vote in the Tennessee House was 50–49 in favor, with the winning vote provided by a representative thought to be a possible no vote but who was swayed by a letter he carried in his pocket from his widowed mother urging him to support woman suffrage.

Q. What place is considered the home of the modern gay rights movement?

A. The Stonewall Inn in New York City's Greenwich Village. After police raided the popular gay night club on June 28, 1969, patrons for the first time protested and fought back violently. Although police got the riot under control, it started again the following night. A Gay Pride march on Christopher Street celebrated the first anniversary of the riots, and today the last weekend of June sees Gay Pride events throughout the world.

Q. Where did world-famous African American opera singer Marian Anderson sing on April 9, 1939?

A. The Lincoln Memorial. Born in Philadelphia, Anderson had been successful in her home country, but after touring Europe in the 1930s, she had a chance to be a superstar in the United States. However, segregationist policies caused the Daughters of the American Revolution (DAR) to refuse to allow her to perform in Constitution Hall, which the organization owned. Controversy raged, leading First Lady Eleanor Roosevelt to resign from the DAR and help set up the dramatic and historic free concert performed to a mixed-race crowd at the base of the Lincoln Memorial.

Q. The 1968 Democratic National Convention was perhaps more memorable for what happened outside the convention hall than what happened inside, as youthful protesters fought police in the streets. What city hosted the Democrats in 1968?

A. Chicago. With the nation divided by the Vietnam War and the assassinations of Martin Luther King Jr. and Robert F. Kennedy fueling animosity, the city became a battleground for antiwar protests. Confrontations between protesters and police turned violent, and Americans witnessed it all on national TV.

AMERICANA

★ ★ ★ ★ ★ ★ ★ ★ ★ ★ ★ ★ ★

What makes up America—its woof and warp, the roads and rivers that weave together and bind the fabric of this great land—can be called Americana. These questions—about the essence of the nation—thread through the colorful facts that make up a people and its culture.

Q. What is the world's longest shared border between two countries?

A. The 3,987-mile boundary between the United States and Canada, which is for the most part undefended. As western expansion in both countries progressed during the 19th century, the border kept getting extended along the 49th parallel. Stretching into the Strait of Georgia in the Pacific Ocean, the border's location was finalized in 1872.

Q. Where was the coldest temperature ever recorded in the United States?

A. In Prospect Creek Camp, Alaska, where the thermometer plunged to −80 degrees Fahrenheit in 1971. Stanley, Idaho, however, is the coldest place on average in the continental United States. It boasted the coldest temperatures in the nation nearly 400 times between 1995 and 2005. The record in Stanley is −54 degrees Fahrenheit, which it hit on December 23, 1983, but it's not often that it gets *that* cold.

Q. On what street will you find Graceland Mansion?

A. Elvis Presley Boulevard in Memphis. The King of Rock 'n' Roll bought the southern colonial home in 1957 when the street was still called Highway 51 South (the Memphis city council changed the name in June 1971). Graceland was Elvis's family home and private retreat until his death in 1977. In 1982 the Graceland home and tour was opened to the public, and fans got an inside look at Elvis's life, from his

infamous "Jungle Room" den to the Graceland kitchen. In 2006 Graceland was designated a National Historic Landmark. Today the mansion remains one of the country's top tourist attractions, captivating more than 600,000 visitors each year.

Q. During the Dust Bowl of the 1930s, where did farm workers of the Great Plains go?

A. Most traveled along Route 66, making that highway a famous factor in U.S. history. Some stopped to work in Arizona, but most continued on to California, where there were reports of work and opportunity. This migration gathered steam in 1935 and peaked in early 1938. Some 40 percent of these workers and their families headed for Los Angeles, one of the nation's fastest growing cities; many more turned north for the Central Valley, California's produce basket. At one point, 7,000 migrants were pouring into the state every month.

Q. How long was Route 66?

A. Stretching from Chicago, Illinois, into the Midwest, through the Great Plains and the Southwestern desert, to end at the lip of the Pacific coastline at Santa Monica, California, U.S. Route 66 ran 2,248 miles. The long roadway became a romantic icon for open-road auto travel in the '50s and '60s. By the time the U.S. Interstate System replaced Route 66 with super-highways in the '80s, millions of riders had gotten their "kicks on Route 66."

★ The exact geographic center of the continental United States is near the town of Lebanon, Kansas, which is in the far northern portion of the state, just off the Nebraska border. If you want to include Alaska and Hawaii, then the geographic center moves to a point near Castle Rock, South Dakota, in the west-central portion of the state.

Q. This popular entertainment destination was launched in 1941 with a hotel and casino on a desolate road a few miles from town. Can you name it?

A. The Vegas Strip. Before then, the area had hotels and casinos, but the vast majority of them stood on Fremont Street in downtown Las Vegas. But when Tom Hull built his "El Rancho" hotel on a well-traveled stretch of road connecting Vegas to Los Angeles, the hotel prospered and other entrepreneurs were drawn to the cheap land of the new development area.

Q. Which American national park has also been called a "River of Grass"?

A. The Everglades. This beautiful wetlands once covered nearly 11,000 square miles, but human development over the past century

★★★ **FAST FACT** ★★★
Although the first U.S. national park wasn't named until the 1870s, the National Capital Parks, the White House, and the National Mall were all set aside as park land on July 16, 1790.

has cut that down to 4,000 square miles. Everglades National Park, which protects roughly a quarter of the original ecosystem, was created in 1947. Since that time, the Everglades has been named a World Heritage Site, a Biosphere Reserve, and a Wetlands of International Importance.

"There can be nothing in the world more beautiful than the Yosemite, the groves of the giant sequoias and redwoods, the Canyon of the Colorado, the Canyon of the Yellowstone, the Three Tetons; and our people should see to it that they are preserved for their children and their children's children forever, with their majestic beauty all unmarred."

—Teddy Roosevelt

Q. How large is the Great Plains?

The Ten Largest U.S. Cities, 1800

★ ★ ★ ★ ★ ★ ★ ★ ★ ★ ★

1. New York City, New York	60,515
2. Philadelphia, Pennsylvania	41,220
3. Baltimore, Maryland	26,514
4. Boston town, Massachusetts	24,937
5. Charleston, South Carolina	18,824
6. Northern Liberties township, Pennsylvania*	10,718
7. Southwark district, Pennsylvania*	9,621
8. Salem town, Massachusetts	9,457
9. Providence town, Rhode Island	7,614
10. Norfolk borough, Virginia	6,926

Northern Liberties and Southwark were both annexed by Philadelphia in 1854.

A. Covering parts of the states of Kansas, Nebraska, Montana, North Dakota, South Dakota, Colorado, Texas, Wyoming, and Oklahoma, all in all, the Great Plains totals some 500,000 square miles of land—nearly 15 percent of the continental United States.

Q. A swath of the Great Plains has gained a nickname from the storms that occur there. What is it?

A. Tornado Alley. Most maps define this as an area through the Great Plains stretching from the Texas panhandle up through Nebraska, Oklahoma, and Kansas. Some tornado experts include Illinois, Iowa, and Indiana on their maps; others include southeastern states such as Georgia and Mississippi. On May 3, 1999, a total of 74 tornadoes touched down in Oklahoma. Some of these passed through Oklahoma City and its suburbs, killing 46 people, injuring 800, and causing $1.5 billion in damage.

Q. Name the Great Lakes.

A. From east to west: Erie, Ontario, Huron, Michigan, and Superior. The Great Lakes were an important part of the expansion of the early United States, providing a waterway for transporting goods and people; the lakes became a major channel for immigrants heading westward from New England and New York. These immigrants built major cities along the coasts of the lakes, including Cleveland on Lake Erie and Chicago on Lake Michigan.

> ★★★ **FAST FACT** ★★★
> Lake Michigan was once known as "Lake of the Stinking Water."

Q. Cleveland, Ohio, is home to the Rock and Roll Hall of Fame and Museum. Why Cleveland?

A. Cities such as New York, Memphis, New Orleans, Detroit, and Chicago were all in the running to house the Rock and Roll Hall of Fame and Museum, but in the end, Cleveland won out, and the Hall of Fame opened there in 1995. After all, it was Cleveland disc jockey Alan Freed who first coined the term *rock 'n' roll* in 1954, and the city was also the location of the first rock 'n' roll concert. Nostalgia aside, Cleveland may have been chosen because its civic leaders offered the best financial package.

Q. Who made the first cross-country automobile trip?

A. Horatio Nelson Jackson. Over drinks at a genteel club in 1903, Jackson made a $50 bet that he could drive an automobile from San Francisco to New York. This was no mean feat: Gas stations did not yet exist, and there were only 150 miles of paved roads in the entire country. Jackson proved it could be done, though he spent 63 days and a great deal of his wife's money doing it.

TRUE OR FALSE The American Interstate Highway System was inspired by a trip Dwight Eisenhower took in 1919.

ANSWER True. Lieutenant Colonel Dwight Eisenhower took part in a convoy of Army trucks, tanks, motorcycles, and other military vehicles that left Washington, D.C., bound for San Francisco. The arduous slog across rickety bridges and unfit thoroughfares took several weeks. Motivated partially by this painful experience and partially by the massive autobahns he had seen in Germany after World War II, Eisenhower became a forceful advocate for the creation of a state-of-the-art Interstate Highway System when he was elected president 33 years later.

Q. In 1911 the New Jersey–based Nestor Film Company leased a vacant tavern in downtown Hollywood to use as a studio. In less than three months more than a dozen other studios had set up shop in Hollywood, leasing properties along Sunset Boulevard.

What had Hollywood been known for before this?

A. Once little more than a dusty stretch of land populated by the Cahuenga Indians, and later by Spanish Franciscan missionaries, the area had seen a prominent fruit industry arise in the temperate climate. It was known as a city of lemons and figs.

Q. Edwin S. Porter's *The Great Train Robbery,* released in 1903, is often considered the first Western movie. Where was it shot?

A. In the wilds of New Jersey. Only about a dozen minutes long, this is a milestone in film history. In addition to being the first western, it was one of the very first movies to have a narrative with a beginning, middle, and end. It also set a standard of sensationalism that the movies have never given up. In one scene, a bandit points his gun at the camera and fires, frightening viewers of this new medium who weren't necessarily sure whether a real bullet was coming toward them or not.

Q. What is the highest point in North America?

A. Mount McKinley, which rises some 20,000 feet out of the glacial ranges of south-central Alaska. First spotted by European explorers in 1794, the mountain had played an important role in Native American cultures for thousands of

★★★ **FAST FACT** ★★★

The first person to climb Mount McKinley solo was Naomi Uemura, a Japanese adventurer, who accomplished his feat in August 1970.

years. It was particularly significant to the Athapaskan people, who referred to the mountain as Denali ("The High One").

Q. Why is the Great Salt Lake salty?

A. It is due to the fact that it is a *terminal* lake. Most freshwater lakes have an outlet, such as a river or a channel to a larger body of water. The Great Salt Lake has no such outlet, and without one there is nowhere for the minerals in the lake to go. The water evaporates, but the minerals stay behind, becoming more concentrated as the next hydrological cycle begins. Salt production in the area became a major industry when some of the earliest American settlers recognized the value of the minerals in the lake. That industry continues to be the driving economic force in the Great Salt Lake region, with companies such as Morton Salt extracting nearly two million tons of salt from the lake each year.

Q. On average, what is the warmest location in the nation?

A. The most consistently warm place in the United States is Key West, Florida, which has an average daily temperature of 78.1 degrees

★★★ **FAST FACT** ★★★

The highest temperature ever recorded in the United States was 134 degrees Fahrenheit at Greenland Ranch in Death Valley, California, in 1913.

Fahrenheit year-round. Key West also boasts sunshine 76 percent of the time.

Q. The intersection of Broadway and Seventh Avenue, in the heart of Manhattan, is more commonly known by what name?

A. Times Square. It had earlier been called Long Acre Square, but in 1904 the *New York Times* moved its headquarters there and renamed it Times Square. In that same year the *Times* held a massive New Year's celebration in the square, a tradition that is carried on today.

Q. How long is the Mississippi River?

A. The Mississippi River begins in northern Minnesota at Lake Itasca and winds 2,552 miles south before emptying into the Gulf of Mexico near New Orleans. When the area around the river was first settled, farmers could send their grain down the Mississippi to be sold, or even through New Orleans to

The Ten Largest U.S. Cities, 1900

★ ★ ★ ★ ★ ★ ★ ★ ★ ★ ★ ★

1. New York City, New York	3,437,202
2. Chicago, Illinois	1,698,575
3. Philadelphia, Pennsylvania	1,293,697
4. St. Louis, Missouri	575,238
5. Boston, Massachusetts	560,892
6. Baltimore, Maryland	508,957
7. Cleveland, Ohio	381,768
8. Buffalo, New York	352,387
9. San Francisco, California	342,782
10. Cincinnati, Ohio	325,902

markets overseas, but the river's currents were so powerful that it was impractical to make the reverse trip. With the advent of the steamboat, however, people could sail upstream, and trips that had taken months to complete could be made in a matter of days. The cost of shipping goods upriver decreased by a factor of ten.

Q. Where can you wade across the mighty Mississippi River?

A. At its source, Lake Itasca. The river there is just inches deep and a few feet wide. Wading across it is child's play!

Q. In June 1933, Camden, New Jersey, introduced a brand-new way of watching movies. What was it?

A. The drive-in. A month earlier, Richard Hollingshead Jr. had received a U.S. patent for his design to watch movies from your car, and he built the first such "theater" in Camden. The initial offering was *Wives Beware*, starring Adolphe Menjou, which entertained more than 600 viewers. Drive-ins became notorious for those who wanted to do more in their cars than simply watch the movie. Hollingshead's design  eventually led to more than 3,000 "passion pits" (as the outdoor theaters were sometimes called) at their peak in the late 1950s.

★ The saguaro cactus is arguably the best-known symbol of the American Southwest. Native only to the Sonoran Desert, which stretches from southern Arizona to northern Mexico, the saguaro has an average life span of 150 years, with some specimens living for more than two centuries.

Q. How did Death Valley get its forbidding name?

A. It is one of the harshest deserts in the world. The first American settlers reached the area during the gold rush of 1849. Two groups of these settlers got lost and wandered through the region for months without a map. Miraculously, only one person died.

> ★★★ **FAST FACT** ★★★
> Death Valley saw no rain in 1929 and a total of only 0.64 inch over a period of 40 months from 1931 to 1934.

Q. What was the first significant country music radio program, and from where did it originate?

A. *National Barn Dance* on WLS in Chicago. Begun by George D. Hay, its first broadcast was on April 19, 1924, and it ran on the station for 36 years. George D. Hay didn't remain there during that entire time, though. Just over a year after the show debuted, Hay left to go to Nashville, Tennessee, where he started the *WSM Barn Dance*, which later became known as *The Grand Ole Opry*.

Q. During the 1960s and early '70s, NASA rockets took off from Cape Kennedy, but today, there is no such place. Where was it?

A. Cape Canaveral. The Spanish gave this Florida cape the name Canaveral in the 1500s. After President John F. Kennedy was assassinated in 1963, his widow, Jackie Kennedy, suggested to new President Lyndon Johnson that the cape might be an appropriate place to honor the leader who had initiated the

The Ten Largest U.S. Cities, 2010

* * * * * * * * * * * *

1. New York City, New York	8,175,133
2. Los Angeles, California	3,792,621
3. Chicago, Illinois	2,695,598
4. Houston, Texas	2,099,451
5. Philadelphia, Pennsylvania	1,526,006
6. Phoenix, Arizona	1,445,632
7. San Antonio, Texas	1,327,407
8. San Diego, California	1,307,402
9. Dallas, Texas	1,197,816
10. San Jose, California	945,942

effort to send a manned flight to the moon. Johnson had the cape, and the space center it housed, renamed for Kennedy, but local Floridians were unhappy with the change. It took them ten years, but residents convinced the Florida legislature to give the cape its old name back. Never fear, though. The space center on Cape Canaveral still holds the slain president's name.

Q. The Ringling Brothers started their traveling circus in 1884. Where did the circus go when it wasn't traveling?

A. Baraboo, Wisconsin, in an enclave they called Ringlingville. Starting out small, this circus stayed within the northern Midwest region, but by the 1890s it had become one of the largest circuses in the country. In 1889 the Ringlings bought train cars and began traveling by rail, which extended their range considerably. In 1919, however, the attraction merged with the Barnum & Bailey Greatest Show on Earth and moved to join that group's winter quarters in Bridgeport, Connecticut.